the dodo

Starfish's STORY

The True Story of How One Little Puppy Learned to Walk

BY BONNIE BADER

SCHOLASTIC INC.

Photo credits: Cover and all images in photo insert: © The Gray Family.
Stock images: © Shutterstock.com

Copyright © 2023, Vox Media, LLC.
THE DODO is a registered trademark of Vox Media, LLC. All Rights Reserved.

All rights reserved. Published by Scholastic Inc., *Publishers since 1920*. SCHOLASTIC and associated logos are trademarks and/or registered trademarks of Scholastic Inc.

ISBN 978-1-339-01241-4

10 9 8 7 6 5 4 3 2 1   23 24 25 26 27
Printed in the U.S.A.   40
First printing 2023
Book design by Jennifer Rinaldi

CONTENTS

1. Found 1

2. Hope 11

3. Finding a Foster 17

4. Surgery 31

5. Recovery 39

6. Lost and Found 49

7. Feet on the Ground 57

8. Rehabbing Starfish 77

9. A Surprise Call 93

10. The Video Goes Viral 99

11. A Setback 109

12. Funding Starfish 119

13. Putting Starfish Back Together Again . . . 129

14. One Recovery Is Not Enough 137

15. Three Times Lucky 149

16. Strengthening Starfish 161

17. *The Dodo*—Again! 175

18. Epilogue 187

More About Friends of the Alameda
Animal Shelter 191

How to Help Dogs at an Animal Shelter 195

Is Your Family Ready to Foster a Dog? 199

CHAPTER 1

FOUND

WHEN ALAINA ONESKO RECEIVED A
call that someone spotted an abandoned puppy
on Crown Beach in Alameda, California, she
hopped in her truck. As an animal control
officer, it was Alaina's job to help lost, abandoned, and injured animals. She didn't know
the condition of this puppy. All she knew was

the puppy had been left alone on the beach in a cardboard box. There was no time to waste.

It was October 4, 2017. When Alaina arrived at the location, she walked on the beach, her shoes leaving deep prints along the shoreline. It was a beautiful day; the sun was shining and paragliders were zipping along the water.

Alaina spotted the cardboard box. It had been turned on its side, and Alaina saw two little ears sticking out. But where was the rest of the puppy?

"Oh, my," Alaina said, bending down. "What do we have here?" Alaina straightened out the box.

A puppy was indeed inside, lying on top of some dried dog food. But this puppy was different. Her legs were splayed out around her tiny body. She looked as flat as a pancake!

The puppy tipped her head and looked up at the woman. *Hi there. I was just left here, alone in this box. I can't get out and I'm kind of scared. I think I'm at the beach. I can smell the salt water. And some sand is stuck in my ears. You look nice. I'm nice, too! Can you help me?*

Alaina picked up the puppy and put the dog against her chest.

"It's okay, little one," Alaina said. "I've got you now."

Fearing that the puppy was injured, Alaina bundled her up and drove straight to a veterinarian's office. She hoped that the people who worked there would be able to help this little doggie.

Are you taking me home? the puppy wondered? *I could really use something to eat. And I could probably use a bath, too!*

Alaina parked her car and carefully carried the puppy inside.

"I found her at Crown Beach," Alaina explained to the receptionist.

The puppy gazed at Alaina with eager eyes as she talked.

"I'm worried she's hurt," Alaina continued. "Look at her legs. She looks like a starfish."

"Starfish!" a volunteer who was standing nearby said. "I think that's what you should call her."

The receptionist called the vet and soon ushered Alaina and Starfish inside the examination room.

This table is hard and cold, Starfish thought. *But the people around me look nice and friendly, so I don't feel so scared anymore. Maybe they'll take me to their home!*

The vet felt Starfish's legs.

She touched Starfish's tummy.

She examined Starfish's mouth.

She ran her hands up and down Starfish's spine.

"Well, what I can say is that this is a Belgian Malinois puppy. And she's probably about ten weeks old. I think we should get an ultrasound. Maybe that test will help us figure out why she's so . . . flat."

Alaina waited nervously as Starfish was taken away for the ultrasound, which would allow the vet to see the organs inside the puppy's body.

As Alaina waited, she wondered what could have happened to this cute little pup. Had she been hit by a car? Maybe, but Alaina didn't notice any blood, and the dog didn't seem to be in any pain. But she had never seen a flat puppy before.

Alaina shook her head. Who could have abandoned this helpless puppy?

A little later, the vet returned. Starfish was wagging her tail. But the vet didn't look happy.

"I think this puppy was born with some kind of birth defect," the vet reported. "It looks like her internal organs didn't develop properly."

"Is that why she's so flat?" Alaina asked.

The vet nodded. Then she told Alaina the puppy probably wouldn't live very long.

Tears began to form in Alaina's eyes. "Is there any way to help her?"

The vet slowly shook her head. "I'm afraid not."

Sadly, Alaina picked up the puppy. The

little animal nuzzled against Alaina's chest, her tail still wagging. *She seems so alive and happy*, Alaina thought. *I want her to be able to live a full and happy life.*

Alaina knew that their next stop was the Friends of the Alameda Animal Shelter (FAAS). The people who worked there would decide what to do.

~

As soon as Alaina walked into FAAS, she heard the yipping, barking, and meowing of the animals waiting to be fostered or adopted.

"Who have you brought us today?" Steve Ferguson, the shelter's director of operations asked.

Alaina gingerly placed the puppy down.

The staff gasped when they saw that the puppy couldn't stand on her legs.

"I'm calling her Starfish," Alaina said.

"What a perfect name!" Steve agreed.

"Poor little thing," a volunteer said, reaching down to scratch the puppy behind her ears. "Do you think she's in pain?"

Alaina shrugged. "If she is, she's not showing it," Alaina said, motioning to the puppy's wagging tail.

"But I bet you're hungry and thirsty," Steve said. He quickly placed bowls of food and water in front of the puppy.

After Starfish ate, Alaina brought her into the examination room. There, Kim, one of the techs, waited.

Kim, Steve, and Alaina thought Starfish looked so happy. There had to be something they could do to help her. As they stood around the little flat puppy with the bright eyes and wagging tail, they began to cry. They desperately wanted to save her.

"We need to call John," Steve said, wiping his eyes. "Maybe he'll know what to do."

John, the shelter's director, was out of the office for the day on business. But when they finally reached him, John heard crying in the background. "I know you've seen really sick puppies before," John said. "Why all the crying this time?"

Steve sniffled. "I–I don't know," he said. "This puppy is just so cute. And happy. And, well, *alive*."

John didn't say anything for a minute. And although he had a very busy day planned, he knew he had to get back to the shelter to see this puppy. "Give me twenty minutes," John said. And he hung up the phone.

"Don't do anything," Steve said. "We have to wait for John."

Alaina breathed a big sigh of relief. Maybe John would figure out some way to save this little puppy.

CHAPTER 2

HOPE

BREATHLESSLY, JOHN LIPP RACED into Starfish's examination room at FAAS. He looked at the little pup splayed out on the table and his heart melted.

Starfish gazed at him with her dark eyes.

Deep down inside, John felt that there was something very special about Starfish.

As John picked her up, he felt a tingle going up and down his spine.

Oh, look: another friend! Starfish thought. *Mmm, he smells so nice. I'm going to give him a big, sloppy kiss!*

John hugged the puppy close. "There's something different about this one," he said. "It's like she has a spark of life inside her. I think we should get a second opinion."

Everyone in the room wiped their tears and smiled. Perhaps there was some hope after all.

～

With money from FAAS's Angel Fund, they were able to take Starfish to another veterinarian's office for a second opinion. The Angel Fund is an emergency source of money that has helped save over two hundred animals at

FAAS. Hopefully, the second vet would know what was wrong with Starfish so that he could help her.

"Oh, you are so fragile," Alaina said, as she put Starfish in her truck.

Starfish struggled to stand up to get a look outside the window. But her floppy legs couldn't support her.

As soon as they arrived at the vet's office, Alaina ran inside with Starfish. She knew there was no time to waste.

The vet quickly ushered Starfish into the examination room.

He gently touched Starfish's legs and tried to get her to stand.

But Starfish just flopped back down, her legs splayed around her.

Then the vet carefully pressed on Starfish's

stomach to feel her organs. And then he felt her muscles.

Soon, the vet was done with his examination. He was ready to give a diagnosis. Alaina held her breath.

"I believe this dog is suffering from something called swimmer puppy syndrome, or SPS," the vet explained.

"What exactly does that mean?" Alaina asked.

"It's a rare condition that affects the dog's adductor muscles." The vet pointed to Starfish's inner thighs. Then he explained that these muscles would normally help Starfish stand. But in her case, they were too weak. That was why she was so floppy.

"What do you think caused it?" Alaina wanted to know.

The vet shook his head. "We're not sure."

He went on to explain that some people think an infection carried by the dog's mother when she is pregnant could be responsible. Others suspect this syndrome occurs when puppies are kept in small crates and can't move around. When this happens, their muscles don't develop properly.

Alaina reached down to scratch Starfish behind her ears. Starfish wriggled and waggled. "Is there a cure?" she asked.

The vet nodded. "She could learn to walk. But only with early intervention."

The vet told Alaina that Starfish would have to undergo intense physical therapy (PT) to strengthen her muscles and legs.

Alaina was relieved. And happy! Perhaps there was a way for Starfish to have a full and happy life after all. But Alaina knew they would have to start the therapy as soon as possible. The vet told her that most puppies with this syndrome start at a few weeks old. Starfish was already about ten weeks.

Hopefully, it wasn't too late.

CHAPTER 3
FINDING A FOSTER

WHEN ALAINA AND STARFISH arrived back at FAAS, John told her some news. "The vet just took another look at Starfish's ultrasound. She has two hernias."

A hernia is a hole or a weak section in the stomach's muscle wall. This hole allows the contents of a dog's stomach to leak out into the abdomen. Only surgery can repair a hernia.

Alaina was worried when she heard that Starfish needed hernia surgery. "The vet said she needs PT as soon as possible," Alaina told Steve and John as they sat around John's desk. "I really don't think we have time to wait."

"But she also needs the hernia repair," John said.

"Which should be done first?" Steve asked.

"Since she'll need to recover from the hernia surgery, I think it makes sense to do that first," John decided.

Alaina nodded. "I see your point. This way, she'll be healed and rested by the time her PT starts."

Steve went into his office to call the veterinary hospital to see when they could schedule Starfish for the hernia surgery.

Alaina cuddled Starfish in her arms. "Don't worry, little one. We'll get you fixed up real fast. Then you'll learn to walk!"

A few minutes later, Steve returned to John's office. "I have good news and bad news."

"Good news first?" Alaina said.

"The good news is that the hospital has a surgeon who can perform Starfish's surgery," Steve said.

"And the bad news?" John asked.

"The bad news is that the surgery can't be scheduled for a few days . . ." Steve said.

"And we really can't hold Starfish here for that time," John guessed.

The group knew what this meant. Since FAAS is primarily a shelter, it couldn't keep Starfish until her surgery and care for her while she recovered. That meant they had to find Starfish a foster home. A foster family would temporarily care for Starfish until she was healthy enough to find a forever home.

But finding a foster home for this special puppy would be tricky. Still, Steve sent out emails to a list of people who had fostered animals in the past. Hopefully, someone would be willing to open their home to Starfish.

Ding!

The email alert on Liam Gray's computer rang. It was a message from FAAS asking if he and his family would foster a puppy.

Although the Gray family had fostered many animals from the shelter in the past, Liam wasn't too sure about this one. This puppy couldn't walk. And she had to wear diapers since she couldn't stand up to go to the bathroom. Although Liam really did want to help, he thought this one was a no. He didn't think that his busy family of five had the time to devote to this special pup.

Just then, Liam's thirteen-year-old, Maggie, walked into the room and looked over his shoulder. A photo of Starfish stared back at them, immediately melting their heart.

"Oh my gosh!" Maggie exclaimed, pushing their reddish-brown hair behind their ears. "That puppy is so cute!"

Liam smiled. "She is, but . . ."

"Does she need a foster home?" Maggie asked anxiously.

Liam nodded. "She does, but this puppy will require a lot of work."

"I can do it!" Maggie exclaimed without missing a beat.

Liam sighed. He knew Maggie was responsible, but this puppy would need constant attention.

"You'll have to watch her *all* the time," Liam told Maggie. "And that includes feeding her and changing her diapers."

"I'm one hundred percent up for it," Maggie said.

"Well, it is only for a couple of days," Liam said, considering the situation.

Maggie jumped up and down. "Yes! When do we get to meet her?"

Liam smiled. "Let me talk it over with your mom."

Back at the shelter, Starfish lay anxiously inside a kennel. All around her, dogs were barking and crying. She was pretty sure she could hear some cats meowing, too. And although all the people who worked at the shelter were super nice to her, Starfish just wanted to go *home*. Wherever that home might be.

Just then, Starfish heard footsteps approaching. She cocked her head and wagged her tail. It was a family! And they stopped right in front of her crate.

Starfish locked eyes with the red-headed child in the family called Maggie.

Hi, Maggie! Are you going to take me home? I heard I can learn to walk. And I promise I'll try really, really hard!

"She is the most precious thing in the entire world!" Maggie said, bending down to get a better look at Starfish. "She looks like a little teddy bear."

"And look at how she's wriggling around,"

said Maggie's mom, Leigh Anne. "She's so happy to see us!"

Maggie's siblings, five-year-old Oliver and eleven-year-old Sarah, also bent down to pet Starfish.

"I can help, Maggie," Oliver said.

"Me too," Sarah added.

Maggie's parents nodded in agreement.

"Starfish will be primarily Maggie's responsibility," Liam said. "But I'm sure Maggie will appreciate your help."

"Definitely," Maggie said.

"Remember, Maggie, we're just fostering her for a couple of days," Leigh Anne reminded her.

"Uh-huh," Maggie said, only half listening as they picked up Starfish.

Mmm . . . you smell nice, Maggie. And your

hair is so soft. I'm just going to nuzzle my nose right here and stay forever!

It was love at first sight.

~~~

"Here's your new home," Maggie said as they carried Starfish inside their house.

"*Temporary* home," Liam reminded them.

Maggie rolled their eyes and giggled. "We'll see about that."

Maggie gave Starfish a tour of the house so she'd feel comfortable, even though Maggie knew Starfish wouldn't be going anywhere without them. Maggie showed the puppy the kitchen, the living room, and the bedrooms.

"And this is Pearl," Maggie said. They bent down so the kitten could get a good look at Starfish. Maggie's family had recently adopted Pearl from FAAS.

Pearl hissed and arched her back. But Starfish seemed interested.

Hi! Didn't I just see you at the shelter? No? Well, it was a kitty that looked just like you! Wanna play?

Pearl just lifted her nose and trotted away.

~~~

For the next couple of days, Maggie brought Starfish with them wherever they went. Starfish didn't need any special care—just love. And Maggie gave her plenty of that!

"Even though I'm on school vacation, I have to get some homework done," Maggie said, picking up Starfish. Then Maggie gently plopped her on the bed. Starfish snuggled up next to Maggie as they scrolled through their assignments. Maggie's bed was so warm and cozy that Starfish fell into a deep sleep.

"Break time!" Maggie said later, scooping up Starfish and taking her outside.

Sarah and Oliver were on the front lawn kicking around a soccer ball.

"Hey, Starfish!" Oliver exclaimed. "Wanna play?"

"Well, she can't exactly play soccer," Sarah said.

"I know that," Oliver said. "We can play a sitting-down game."

Maggie giggled and set Starfish down next to Oliver. Starfish started to move her front and hind legs even though her body remained flat on the ground.

"It looks like she's trying to swim!" Sarah said.

Maggie nodded. "That's exactly why they call her condition swimmer puppy syndrome."

"What do you think will happen to her?" Oliver asked, tickling Starfish's nose with a leaf.

"After her surgery she'll start therapy to help her learn to walk," Maggie said.

"I mean, where will she *live*?" Oliver asked.

"Yeah," Sarah added. "Mom and Dad said we can only keep her until the surgery."

Maggie's heart began to race. They knew they couldn't give up Starfish now. It had only been a few days, but they had grown so attached to this little puppy.

"Can you keep an eye on her for a second?" Maggie asked their siblings. "There's something I have to do."

Maggie raced up the front stairs to their house and swung open the door. "Mom! Dad! I need to talk to you!"

Maggie's parents ran to the front door. "Is everything okay?" Leigh Anne asked. "Did something happen to Starfish?"

Maggie shook their head. "She's fine. For now. But I worry about what's going to happen to her after her surgery."

"Maggie, you know we said we'd just foster Starfish until her hernia repair," Liam said.

Tears began to form in Maggie's eyes. "I know. But I just love her so much. I can't let her go."

"We're all getting attached to her," Leigh Anne said. "But her therapy is going to be a lot of work."

"I love her so much that I start crying whenever I think about her leaving," Maggie passionately told their parents.

Liam and Leigh Anne looked at each other

and sighed. "Right now, we're just her foster family. Let's get through Starfish's surgery first. Then we'll talk about the future."

Maggie's heart skipped a beat. Was there a chance that Starfish could really become part of their family—for good?

CHAPTER 4

SURGERY

BUZZ! BUZZ!

Maggie rolled over to shut off their alarm and pulled the covers over their head. *Why do I have to get up so early?*

Then they shot up in bed. Today was the day Maggie and their mom were bringing Starfish to the vet for her surgery!

Quickly, Maggie got dressed. Then they looked around for Starfish. But Maggie couldn't find her.

"Starfish?" Maggie called, even though they knew the puppy couldn't come running.

"Mom? Dad? Where's Starfish?" Maggie started to panic.

"Your mom already has her in the car, sleepyhead," Liam said. "Now hurry up, or they'll leave without you!"

Maggie raced out to the car and opened the door. Starfish wagged her tail. Maggie scooped up the puppy, put her on their lap, and they were off.

~

I love you so much, Maggie! And you've been taking such good care of me! I love snuggling in your bed. I love playing outside with you, Sarah, and

Oliver. And I really love giving you kisses. (I love the ones you give me, too!) Where are we going now? Never mind. I don't need to know. I'll follow you anywhere!

~

Leigh Anne parked the car in front of the shelter, and Maggie carried Starfish inside.

"I'm so nervous," Maggie said. Their teeth were chattering even though it wasn't cold.

"Don't worry," Leigh Anne said. "This is a routine surgery."

"But Starfish isn't your routine kind of dog," Maggie pointed out.

"You're right," Leigh Anne said. "She's an extraordinarily strong and brave dog. And she'll be just fine."

Maggie managed a smile. But deep down inside, Maggie was still a nervous wreck.

Starfish greeted the staff at the shelter with her usual enthusiasm. Just then, Alaina and Steve came rushing over to them.

"We came early because we wanted to wish Starfish luck," Alaina said.

Starfish wagged her tail.

Maggie and Leigh Anne looked at Alaina in surprise. Why was she here? She should have been on patrol for abandoned animals.

"Don't look so surprised," Alaina said. "I love Starfish, too. I wanted to be here to support Starfish. And your family."

"Team Starfish!" Maggie said, managing a smile.

"She's in good hands," Steve reassured them.

It was time for Maggie and Leigh Anne to go. The team at the shelter would take

Starfish to and from the surgery, and Maggie and Leigh Anne would come back a few hours later to bring Starfish home.

"I know," Maggie said. "One last kiss. For good luck!" Maggie kissed Starfish on her nose.

I'll miss you, Starfish, Maggie thought. *And I know you'll miss me, too. But I'll be right here when you get back.*

~~~

Starfish lay on a cold metal table, faceup. Some cold liquid was spread on her belly.

Where am I? What's that buzzing thing that's tickling me? And why couldn't Maggie be in here with me? They always . . .

And with that last thought, Starfish was fast asleep.

~~~

"Oh, my baby!" Maggie cried with outstretched arms when they were reunited with Starfish later that day.

Is that you, Maggie? Starfish thought. *I can't see you very clearly. Everything looks very blurry. Is it from the medicine the doctor gave me? And what is this thing around my head? I look like an ice-cream cone! And, oh, does my belly hurt!*

"Starfish! I'm so glad you're okay!" Alaina said. "But I knew you would be—you're such a strong little puppy."

Steve gave Starfish a gentle pet on the back, careful not to touch her bandages.

"You'll have to keep her quiet and pretty still for the next ten days," Steve told Leigh Anne and Maggie. "And try to restrict her movement so her stitches will heal."

Leigh Anne and Maggie laughed.

"What's so funny?" Steve asked.

"Um, she can't exactly walk around under normal circumstances," Maggie said.

"Of course not. I'm sorry."

"No worries," Leigh Anne said.

"But Mom, there *is* a worry," Maggie said.

Leigh Anne gave Maggie a quizzical look.

"Starfish has to start her PT as soon as possible," Maggie said. "Do we have ten days to wait?"

"It's important for Starfish to fully recover before she begins the next step in her rehabilitation," Alaina explained.

But Alaina's words didn't comfort Maggie; they still looked anxious.

Leigh Anne put her arm around Maggie's shoulder. "Maggie, I know you're worried, but we have to follow the vet's orders."

"But I'm so scared that her recovery will take too long," Maggie said. "I want to start helping Starfish *now* with physical therapy."

"I know you do," Leigh Anne said. "But right now, the best medicine we can give Starfish is rest. And love."

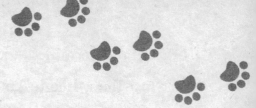

CHAPTER 5

RECOVERY

LIAM, SARAH, AND OLIVER WAITED anxiously on the front steps of their house for Starfish to return.

"I hope the surgery went okay," Oliver said, bouncing up and down nervously.

Liam nodded. "Me too. But I'm sure she's just fine. Starfish is a strong little pup."

"And determined, too," Sarah added.

Just then, Leigh Anne's car pulled into the driveway. The family ran to greet them.

"Is she okay?" Oliver asked when he saw Starfish's bandages.

"She'll be just fine," Leigh Anne reassured her son.

Maggie nuzzled the pup closer as they gently carried her inside the house.

"Don't worry, Starfish," Maggie said. "We're going to take the best possible care of you."

~~~

Pearl came up to sniff Starfish. *Hello, Pearl,* Starfish yawned. *I can't play today. I'm so, so tired. Be careful, Pearl. I have stitches in my tummy. I have to be careful with them, and so do you. I promise I'll play with you when I get better. But all I want to do right now is sleep.*

Starfish looked up at Maggie with her sleepy eyes. *Maggie, can you help explain this to Pearl? I really do need a nap . . .*

Maggie shooed Pearl away and carried Starfish to their room. Then Maggie gently placed Starfish on a white fluffy blanket that was on top of the bed. Starfish's eyes looked so glassy! But Maggie knew it was because the medication the vet gave Starfish hadn't totally worn off. Maggie gently inspected Starfish's wound to see if it looked red or swollen. It didn't seem much different from a couple of hours ago, and Maggie breathed a sigh of relief.

The next time Maggie glanced at Starfish, the puppy was fast asleep.

Maggie took advantage of this downtime to thoroughly read the discharge instructions the vet and the shelter had given them. The next twenty-four hours seemed to be important to Starfish's recovery. Maggie learned that it was normal if Starfish was glassy-eyed (check!), nauseous (not sure), wobbly (she's always wobbly!), shivering (not yet, and hopefully never), or irritable (Maggie doubted that Starfish could ever be irritable).

And although rest was good, Maggie read that they should take Starfish outdoors. Even though she couldn't walk, the fresh air would help with her recovery.

Maggie would do whatever it took to make sure Starfish was okay.

~~~

"Maggie! Time for dinner!" Leigh Anne called.

Maggie opened their eyes and shot up in

bed. They must have fallen asleep alongside Starfish!

And Starfish hadn't woken up at all.

Gently, Maggie rubbed her head. "Come on, Starfish. It's time to try to eat."

Starfish opened one eye. And then the other.

Maggie giggled. "I know you're still sleepy. But I have to try to get some food and water into you."

Maggie carefully carried Starfish to the kitchen.

Starfish's food and water bowl were already filled. And Oliver was sitting on the floor next to them.

"Oliver said the family can't eat until Starfish does," Leigh Anne said.

Maggie smiled. "Go for it, Oliver." Maggie

set Starfish down on the ground next to him.

Oliver held out his little hand with a few bits of kibble in front of Starfish's nose.

Starfish sniffed.

"Come on, girl, you can do it," Oliver coaxed.

Starfish sniffed again. And again.

Finally, she took a piece of kibble and then gobbled up the rest of the food in Oliver's hand. She lapped up some water.

It looked as though Starfish was on the road to recovery!

~

With Maggie's help, Starfish got stronger each day. Maggie checked the puppy's wound daily and looked for any irregular behavior. Maggie also made sure Starfish got plenty of food, water, and rest. And Maggie carried her outside a few times a day so Starfish could get some fresh air.

"So, now that Starfish's surgery is done, can we talk about adopting her?" Maggie asked their parents. "It's almost ten days since her surgery, and she's doing great!"

Liam and Leigh Anne looked at each other.

"We're still not sure," Liam said. "Even though Starfish has recovered nicely from her surgery, she still has a long road of physical therapy ahead of her."

"Well, we knew that from the start," Maggie reasoned.

"Yes, but after some more careful thought, we don't think our family has enough time to devote to helping Starfish learn to walk," Leigh Anne said.

Maggie's eyes welled with tears. "Well, I

don't think we should give up on her," Maggie said, scooping up Starfish and running to their room.

Maggie didn't know what to do. Maggie wasn't old enough to fill out the adoption application on their own. And they didn't know how to convince their parents to change their minds.

Suddenly, Maggie had an idea. They grabbed a pen and paper and wrote:

Dear Mom,

Starfish and I are running away. There is no need to worry, because neither of us are inclined to live in the wilderness of Alameda. We will return to the house as soon as you text us. I decided to leave because there is nothing that hurts me more than imagining life without Starfish, and I want only to be with her.

I love Starfish so much that I cry whenever I think about her leaving and I smile whenever I look at her. It breaks my heart to think that she could be put down or live with someone else.

This escape is more of a symbol than an actual escape. If you want to know where we are, we will be at Franklin Park (I think? The one that has the beach nearby). I am sorry in advance for the pain this causes you. I have food and water for both of us, and Starfish is snuggled up in a backpack. We are okay, we will return after half an hour. I thought that at least, before she leaves, I could pretend that she was

my puppy and I was taking her on a
walk to the park. I could pretend that I
would see her tomorrow and the next
day and the next day and the next all
the way until I go to college, or she dies
of natural causes. I want that more
than anything.

Love,

Maggie

Maggie placed the note on top of their bed
and then quietly opened their bedroom door.
Silently, they tiptoed into the hallway.

The coast was clear.

Quickly, Maggie scampered out the front
door, the backpack with Starfish gently bump-
ing on their back.

And with that, they were gone.

CHAPTER 6

LOST AND FOUND

"MAGGIE! CAN YOU PLEASE JOIN us?" Leigh Anne called. "It's time for a family meeting. We need to talk about Starfish."

There was no reply.

"Maggie!" Leigh Anne called again, growing a bit frustrated.

Nothing.

"Maggie, can you hear me?" Leigh Anne asked.

Still nothing.

Leigh Anne sighed and went to Maggie's room. But Maggie wasn't there. And neither was Starfish.

Leigh Anne walked into Oliver's room. "Have you seen Maggie and Starfish?" she asked her son.

Oliver shook his head. "I've just been in here playing with my toys. I haven't seen them."

Panicking a bit, Leigh Anne ran into Sarah's room. "Have you seen Maggie and Starfish?"

Sarah looked up from her computer and shook her head.

Where could they be?

"What's all the rushing about?" Liam asked.

"Maggie and Starfish are missing!" Leigh Anne said.

"*Missing?*" Liam cried. "Where could they have gone?"

"That's just it," Leigh Anne said, "I don't know!"

~~~

Meanwhile, Starfish was bouncing around in Maggie's backpack. Maggie had unzipped it a bit so Starfish could get some air, but Starfish had no idea where she was.

Maggie, where are we going? I hope you're taking me somewhere fun. But I wish I wasn't inside this bag! Now that I'm practically healed, I want to see what's going on in the world.

As if reading Starfish's thoughts, Maggie said, "Don't worry, Starfish, I'll take you out as soon as we get to the park."

When they arrived, Maggie took Starfish out of the backpack and sat down on a bench. Maggie watched a cute toddler waddle up the blue steps to the slide, then glide down, right into her mom's outstretched arms.

I wonder if my mom found my note. And I wonder how long it will take her to text me.

Maggie knew that they really shouldn't have left home without telling anyone, but they were doing this for Starfish . . . right?

Liam ran outside to check the back and front yards. But there was no sign of Maggie or Starfish. Liam began to panic, too.

"I have no idea where they are," Liam said as he rushed back inside the house.

Just then, Sarah walked downstairs. "Mom, didn't you see this note on Maggie's bed?"

Leigh Anne grabbed the piece of paper from her daughter's hand and read it. Then she breathed a big sigh of relief.

"What does it say?" Liam asked.

Leigh Anne handed the note to her husband, and he read it out loud.

"How long is a half hour?" Oliver wanted to know. "And when will they be back?" Oliver started to cry.

"Don't worry, honey," Leigh Anne said, gathering him up in her arms. "We're going to text Maggie, and they'll be back really, really soon."

Oliver wiped his nose with the back of his sleeve, and Leigh Anne handed him a tissue.

Although Leigh Anne was upset that Maggie had run away, she was relieved that Maggie and Starfish were safe. And she was a little bit impressed by Maggie's devotion to the puppy.

~

Maggie's phone buzzed. It was a text from their mom: *Maggie, you shouldn't have just left. There will be consequences. But please come home. We need to talk.*

Maggie breathed a sigh of relief and stood up. "Well, here goes, Starfish. Hopefully my plan worked."

~

"Maggie! Starfish! You're home!" Oliver shouted a little while later as Maggie ran through the door.

Oliver raced over to Maggie and wrapped his arms around their legs.

Maggie hung their head. "Sorry if I worried you. But I really wanted to get my point across," they told their family. "I don't want to let Starfish go. I want to adopt her."

Liam and Leigh Anne looked at each other.

"We've talked about this already, Maggie," Liam said. "It will be a lot of work getting Starfish back and forth to PT. Plus, I'm sure she'll need to do lots of exercises at home."

"Well, I'm home a lot right now," Leigh Anne said. "So I could take Starfish to rehab."

"And I could go with her!" Oliver said. "And help!"

"And I could be in charge of all the home exercises," Maggie said eagerly.

"And I could try to take her on some walks," Sarah said. "When she's walking, that is."

Liam considered everything his family had said.

Then he slowly nodded.

"Okay, then. We'll continue to foster Starfish until she's recovered. Then we can talk to FAAS about officially adopting her."

The entire family jumped up and down. It looked as though Starfish was going to become part of the Gray family after all!

CHAPTER 7

FEET ON THE GROUND

STARFISH DESPERATELY NEEDED TO start physical therapy. And the Gray family was committed to seeing her rehabilitation through. In addition, FAAS promised to pay the cost of Starfish's therapy. FAAS had recently held a fundraiser, and there was money in their Angel Fund to help.

"Besides, we're part of Team Starfish!" John reminded Leigh Anne.

Starfish's first therapy session was scheduled for Friday, October 20.

"You be a good girl," Maggie told Starfish as they rushed off to school. "And work hard! I'll see you later." Maggie hugged Starfish, put on their backpack, and rushed out the door, followed by their sister and dad.

"It's just you and me today, sport," Leigh Anne said, ruffling Oliver's blond hair.

"And Starfish!" Oliver added. He was going to accompany his mom to Starfish's appointment.

Leigh Anne picked up Starfish, grabbed Oliver's hand, and headed outside. The sky was clear, and the temperature was 60 degrees—a perfect fall day in Alameda!

Oliver scrambled into the back seat of the car. When he was securely buckled in, Leigh Anne lay Starfish on his lap.

"We're going to a place that's going to make you all better!" Oliver told Starfish. "Then we can run and play!"

"She's going to have to work very, very hard at her rehab," Leigh Anne explained. "We don't know whether Starfish will ever be able to really run around. We'll have to be patient with her."

Oliver nodded and gave Starfish a big hug.

Run? Play? Starfish thought. *I want to do that! I know I can do that! I'm going to work really, really hard and never give up. I want to make my new family so, so proud!*

It was a short drive from the Grays' home to the Holistic Veterinary Care and Rehabilitation

Center. Leigh Anne parked the car in front of the one-story building with the orange-and-white striped awning.

Oliver handed Starfish to his mom and then hopped out of the car. He was eager for the therapy to begin!

"Welcome, Starfish!" a cheery receptionist greeted the pup once they got inside.

As soon as Starfish's name was mentioned, a bunch of people crowded around her, including Steve from FAAS. He would be coordinating Starfish's therapy on behalf of the shelter.

"She is *so* cute!" someone remarked.

"And happy!" another person said, noting Starfish's fast-wagging tail.

Just then a man walked through the crowd. "Hello, Starfish," he said with a big smile.

Then he turned to Leigh Anne and Steve. "I'm Dr. Richter, and I'll be supervising Starfish's therapy." He bent down to pat Starfish on her head.

"And you must be Oliver," Dr. Richter said.

Oliver nodded. "I'm here to help Starfish," he told the doctor.

"And I'm so glad," Dr. Richter said. "Why don't you and your mom have a seat while the therapists take Starfish for a little checkup. Then I can explain more about our facility."

Leigh Anne handed over Starfish to the therapists.

Dr. Richter explained to the group that at the Holistic Veterinary Care and Rehabilitation Center, every patient's care is based on their specific needs.

"Oliver, do you know what *holistic* means?" Dr. Richter asked.

Oliver shook his head.

"Holistic therapy means that we don't just treat one part of the dog, we treat the *whole* dog."

Dr. Richter saw that Oliver looked puzzled.

"So, with Starfish, we'll work on her legs and teach her to walk by using obstacle courses, a treadmill, and even swimming," Dr. Richter continued.

Oliver nodded slowly.

"We will also recommend good food for her to eat so she stays healthy. And we might even do something called acupuncture where we stick thin needles into her skin—"

"No!" Oliver shouted. "Please don't hurt Starfish!"

Dr. Richter smiled. "Don't worry, Oliver. Acupuncture doesn't hurt. It actually helps the body heal."

Oliver still looked skeptical.

Starfish was feeling skeptical, too. *Why are these people moving my legs around? It doesn't hurt, but it feels weird. My legs have never moved this much before! And each time they move a leg, they tell me I'm a good girl. Why are they saying this when they're the ones doing all the work? And now they're covering my body with paper. But it feels kinda good . . .*

After the examination, a therapist took Starfish back into the waiting room.

"You can take Starfish home now, and just let her rest for the remainder of the day," Dr. Richter told Leigh Anne and Oliver.

"Today we just moved her legs around a bit. Tomorrow, we'll start the actual therapy to realign her legs and help her gain muscle strength. Leigh Anne, if you have any questions, please feel free to give me a call. You too, Steve."

Steve nodded.

"Thanks, doctor," Leigh Anne said, shaking his hand.

Oliver gave a small wave. It was time to take Starfish home.

~

"Starfish, you're home!" Maggie exclaimed as they ran in the door after school. "How did it go?"

Oliver proudly told Maggie everything that had happened during therapy. He even explained the meaning of the word *holistic*.

Maggie scooped up Starfish and brought her to their room while they did their homework.

I'm so glad to see you, Maggie! Starfish thought. *Therapy wasn't so bad. But now I'm a little sleepy. I think I'm just going to close my eyes for a minute.*

"Sorry to interrupt your beauty rest," Maggie said, gently nudging Starfish a little later. "But it's time to eat."

My tummy's rumbling—let's chow down! I wonder if I'll get a special treat with my dinner tonight!

Maggie carried Starfish downstairs, and after feeding her, Maggie lay the pup on a soft, fluffy dog bed.

After dinner—and a treat!—Maggie took Starfish back up to their room. There the two fell asleep, Starfish snuggled next to Maggie, safe and sound.

~~~

"Okay, this might look like a lot," said one of the two therapists who was working with Starfish the next day. "But it's going to be trial and error at first. It all depends on what she responds to."

Leigh Anne, Oliver, and Steve watched as the therapists rolled up a gray-and-white towel and placed Starfish on top of it.

"Why does her body look very curvy?" Leigh Anne asked.

"Her body curves upward because of her syndrome," the therapist explained. "But it's nothing to worry about. Right now, I want her to get the feel of balancing."

Whoa! Starfish thought as she balanced on

the towel with the therapist's help. *My body isn't flat on the ground anymore. This is fun!*

"You're doing a great job, Starfish!" Leigh Anne encouraged the puppy.

The therapists were impressed. "She's lying on the towel and not putting up a fight!"

"She's such a good girl," Steve agreed. "And so eager to learn."

It was clear that Starfish was responding well to her therapy and she was determined to work hard.

"Now we're going to see if Starfish will still lie on her belly while her legs are off the ground," a therapist explained.

She wrapped a red-and-white striped towel around some foam and placed Starfish on top of it—two legs hanging over the front, and two legs hanging over the back.

The therapist in the back moved Starfish's legs around. "Good job, Starfish!"

"Awesome!" the other therapist exclaimed.

"And she seems to like it, too!" Leigh Anne said, pointing to Starfish's wagging tail.

Whoa, I'm kinda standing on my two front legs. My legs are on the ground! And now my legs are moving! Not by themselves, of course, but with help. This is really, really hard work. But I'm not gonna give up until I can walk—and run—all by myself.

The balancing work continued as the therapists placed Starfish on a yellow squishy ball and moved her legs around. Lying on the ball, Starfish felt less stable than when she was lying on the towels, but she didn't complain or give up. She faced this new challenge and worked harder and harder.

And Starfish was rewarded for all her work—with lots of praise! The sounds of the therapists cheering her on encouraged Starfish to move.

I know what I have to do! Move my head side to side. Move my head up higher. And higher! And now look: I'm almost sitting up all by myself!

Everyone was amazed at how hard Starfish was working at PT. She was making progress faster than anyone had thought possible!

Starfish worked hard at PT, but she also played hard. One day, a puppy was brought in to play with her during her therapy appointment. Since Starfish mostly interacted with humans (and Pearl!), the therapists wanted to get her used to being around other dogs.

Hello! Who are you? You don't look like Pearl.

You look more like me! Anyway, do you want to have some fun? Starfish yapped and squirmed on the towel. The other puppy playfully nipped Starfish on the nose. *Look! I scooted away from you. Come and get me!*

I like you, Starfish thought. *You don't look like Pearl, and you don't act like her, either. Pearl doesn't like to play with me, but you do!*

Leigh Anne laughed as she watched Starfish play. "Look at her go! It seems like she's enjoying her playdate!"

Dr. Richter and the therapists were so impressed with Starfish's progress that they started to post stories about her on the rehab center's Instagram page. The first post showed a video of Starfish lying on the red-and-white striped towel. A therapist held out a treat, and Starfish wiggled over on her belly to grab it:

Meet Starfish! One of our newest (and youngest) patients. Starfish was abandoned in a box and found in Alameda but was happily taken in by the wonderful people at Friends of Alameda Animal Shelter. Starfish has swimmer puppy syndrome, an ailment which prevents a dog's front and hind legs from developing properly. It happens in pups at a young age, and with the right treatment and support there is a great chance of improvement. This was Starfish's first PT appointment.

Immediately, people started following Starfish's progress—the first post about her had almost 1,500 views!

Soon it was time to really help Starfish up on her feet. So, at another therapy session, a therapist put Starfish in a harness. The therapist also fitted Starfish with little pink booties—one on each paw—to keep her from slipping and sliding on the floor. Then the therapists used the harness to help Starfish get up on her feet. Now she was standing on a blue rubber mat!

Oliver sat on the other end of the mat with a treat in his hand. "Come on, Starfish, you can do it," he urged.

I know I can. I know I can. Starfish thought to herself. *Wait, my right leg is up in the air. Where do I put it now? Down on the ground! I moved! Before I was back there, and now I'm closer to Oliver.* Starfish looked back at the therapist again. *What do you want me to do now?* The therapist encouraged Starfish to try again.

I can take another step. Foot up. Then back

down. *I did it! How about another? Foot up. And . . . flop! That's okay. I can get up again. I know I can do it!*

The video of this session was posted on Instagram, too. The therapists captioned the video:

Here's our Starfish at her PT session! So much improvement. Her foster family is doing a great job with the home exercises, which are vital toward seeing improvement. And can we all take a moment and appreciate the AMAZING way she picks herself up at the end?!

~~~

"Okay, Starfish," a therapist said one day during the puppy's PT appointment. "How would you like to try walking underwater?"

Walking? Yes. Starfish thought. *Underwater? I'm not too sure. You're not going to take me to the beach and leave me there, are you?* Starfish looked at the therapist with skeptical eyes.

"You're going to love water treadmill therapy," the therapist said encouragingly.

"Wait," Leigh Anne said. "A treadmill underwater? How does that work?"

"Come along and you'll see," the therapist said, beckoning for Leigh Anne and Oliver to follow her.

Sure enough, they soon found themselves in front of a small tank. Inside the tank, a treadmill was submerged underwater.

"Water therapy puts less stress on an animal's joints, so it's easier and less painful to walk," the therapist explained.

One of the therapists sat in the water and put her hands under Starfish's back for support. This way, Starfish wouldn't tip over to one side. "Just move your legs," she encouraged.

I'm not so sure about this therapy, Starfish said as she pulled back a bit. *I've never been in a pool before. It feels strange, like I'm standing in my water bowl!*

"You can do it," Oliver urged. "I love the water, and I'm sure you will, too! Maybe one day we can swim together!"

Well, if Oliver likes the water, then so do I!

And with that, Starfish took one step. And then another. And before she knew it, she was walking underwater!

Starfish was the little puppy that *could*!

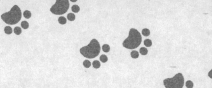

CHAPTER 8

REHABBING STARFISH

ALTHOUGH THE GRAY FAMILY hadn't officially adopted Starfish yet, they were still fully invested in her rehabilitation. They understood that it would take some time before Starfish was strong enough to be medically cleared for adoption.

Starfish had been living with the Grays for

about two months now, and they loved taking care of her. They took her to therapy a few times a week. But they knew they couldn't just rely on the physical therapy appointments if they wanted to get Starfish walking. There was a lot of work to be done at home, too.

Maggie brought Starfish out to the front lawn. "Okay, Starfish, first I'm just going to wrap this towel around your belly."

Whatever you say, Maggie, Starfish thought. *I'm good at following directions!*

"Now, I'm going to pick you up off the ground a little until your legs touch the grass."

Weee! Starfish thought as Maggie held her up. *I can move my legs. Look, Maggie, I'm walking!*

"Hey, everyone, come out here and look at Starfish!" Maggie shouted excitedly.

The family rushed outside.

"It looks like she's walking!" Oliver said, "Even though Maggie is holding her in place."

"She's moving her legs around like crazy," Sarah added. "It's as if she wants to take off and run!"

"Even though she can't run yet, she sure has the motion of running down!" Liam said.

Starfish looked up at Maggie. *Am I doing a good job?*

Maggie scooped Starfish up and gave her a giant hug. "You are such a good girl, Starfish. Great job!"

Starfish gave Maggie a big, sloppy kiss.

~~~

Once Starfish had the *feeling* of what it was like to walk, it was time to teach her to walk without any help. The first step in this phase of her therapy was called *barrier work*. Starfish was held up by her harness and placed between two barriers—one that was black and yellow and one that was blue and black. The barriers acted as walls. So, if Starfish's legs splayed out, they wouldn't go out too far, and she would still feel like she was standing. Using the barriers would give her the feeling that she was walking.

I'm not sure I know what I'm doing! Starfish thought as she struggled to stand, the barriers keeping her legs from totally flopping down. *Please hold on to the harness!*

"You can do it, Starfish!" Leigh Anne urged.

Starfish tried and tried, but she couldn't reach the other side. *That's okay,* Starfish thought. *Everyone falls. But I can get back up! I'm going to try again and again!*

And that's exactly what she did! The next time they tried, yellow hobbles, which look like stretchy exercise bands, were strapped between Starfish's front legs. The hobbles helped keep her legs steady. Then, Starfish was placed in front of a colorful little tunnel, like the kind some babies like to crawl through. Treats were used as an incentive, and it worked: Starfish walked through the tunnel—all by herself!

"Okay, Starfish, are you ready for some barrier work again?" a therapist asked.

Starfish wagged her tail.

"I'll take that as a yes," the therapist said. "But this time you're going to do it on your own!"

The therapist placed Starfish between the two barriers.

Starfish looked up at her. *Where's the harness?*

"I know what you're thinking," the therapist said. "This time, you're going to do it without any help."

"Are you sure she can do this?" Leigh Anne asked.

The therapist nodded. "Today when I was discussing her case with Dr. Richter, he was amazed at her progress. I know things have been moving quickly, but we think she's ready for this next step."

"Okay, if Starfish is ready, so am I," Leigh Anne replied.

Starfish took a step, but her right front leg splayed out.

"That's right Starfish, use the barrier," the therapist said. "It will help you stay upright."

Starfish took another step. And another.

"You can do it!" Oliver encouraged.

Step-by-step, Starfish traveled down the mat until she reached Oliver.

"I'm so proud of you, Starfish!" Leigh Anne said. She gave the puppy a big hug. "Nothing can stop you now!"

Maggie continued to work hard with Starfish at home, too. The rehab center had given the Grays little rubber booties to put on Starfish's paws to help her better grab the ground. But even with the booties, Starfish would slip and slide on the wooden floors inside the house, even when she was held up with a harness.

So, Maggie and Starfish worked mostly outside.

Maggie slipped four pink booties on

Starfish's paws. Then they strapped a pink harness around Starfish's body. "It's always better when you're color coordinated," Maggie said with a laugh.

Carefully, Maggie pulled Starfish up until the dog was standing on her legs.

I feel good, Maggie! I feel strong! I can do it—I know I can! Starfish thought.

Maggie took a deep breath and let go of the harness.

Starfish remained standing.

She didn't fall down!

Maggie was so happy that tears filled their eyes.

"Oh, my goodness, Starfish," Maggie exclaimed. "Look at you!"

And then, plop! Starfish dropped down to the ground. But her tail was still wagging.

Maggie could tell that the puppy felt very proud of herself!

The next time Maggie took Starfish outside, they asked their family to come watch.

"She's getting so strong," Maggie told them. "She can stand by herself."

Sure enough, when Maggie let go of the harness, Starfish stayed on her feet.

"That's amazing, Maggie," Leigh Anne said. "Great job, honey."

"I didn't do anything," Maggie said. "Starfish is doing all the work. She's relentless. She just never gives up!"

Just then, Starfish took a step. And then another step.

"Look!" Sarah said. "Starfish is actually walking!"

"You can do it!" Maggie said as they walked

behind Starfish. In case Starfish fell, Maggie wanted to be right there to catch her.

"Good job, Starfish," Leigh Anne said. "Just take one step at a time."

Starfish stopped for a moment. She turned back to Maggie as if to say, *I've got this!*

The Gray family was so amazed and proud that Starfish was walking by herself.

"I'm with you every step of the way!" Maggie reminded the puppy.

"Oh my gosh, Maggie," Oliver said. "She's going so far!"

Sure enough, Starfish had walked across the entire lawn, leaving the family weeping tears of joy.

~~~

Whether at home or at PT, Starfish continued to work hard. She didn't complain. She didn't bark or whine. Her determination was an inspiration to everyone.

"What is swimmer puppy syndrome?" Holistic Care posted on their Instagram account in November, alongside a video of Starfish walking over long, striped poles, known as cavalletti. Starfish had yellow bands strapped on her legs to help keep her stable while she walked.

"We didn't expect improvement this fast! Her curiosity is definitely showing. Not only is she walking, she's walking over the cavalletti in some land obstacles! Thanks to everyone for your support for little Starfish."

"Going over those cavalletti like a rockstar!" the therapists captioned the video, along with a string of handclapping emojis. *"The amazing journey of Starfish continues to amaze us all every day."*

The clinic's viewers were amazed, too. They left lots of comments on the video:

"WAY TO GO STARFISH!!!! YAHOO!!! You guys are SO AWESOME to help precious Starfish have a great life!"

"So so so so so excited to see Starfish's quick improvement! Seriously warms my heart."

After about two months of therapy, Leigh Anne sat down with Dr. Richter to discuss Starfish's progress. Dr. Richter said that Starfish was one of the hardest working animals in therapy that he had ever seen. He thought that by the end of the month, Starfish wouldn't have to come into the rehab center on a regular basis. But her at-home care would have to continue.

Leigh Anne was so proud of Starfish. As

she watched Starfish on the therapy floor, Leigh Anne thought about how inspiring the puppy was: Starfish worked hard every day and never seemed to give up!

I'm coming. But where do you want me to go? Up that ramp? Easy.

Starfish ran up one side of the ramp and down the other and was rewarded with cheers from the therapists.

"Come on, baby," the therapist urged Starfish to keep going.

I know you want me to finish my workout, but I need to say hello to Dr. Richter first. And look, I'm running all by myself! Hello, Dr. Richter. Starfish gave the doctor a big, sloppy kiss. And Dr. Richter gave her a huge hug.

"Come on, Starfish," Starfish heard.

Okay, okay, I'm coming!

Starfish ran toward a little red, yellow, and blue tunnel and then went straight through it—all by herself. The therapists, along with Leigh Anne, Oliver, and Dr. Richter, were thrilled! Not only was Starfish walking, but she was running, too!

That was fun, but I want to keep going. I'll step over those poles that are between the cones. Over one! Over two! Over three! I did it!

"Great job, Starfish!"

~~~

And then on December 16, the rehabilitation center posted another video:

"Starfish update! Sitting can be difficult with swimmer puppy syndrome, but Starfish nailed it. Thank you to everyone who has been asking about her and for all the love and support."

In the video, Starfish wears a blue harness

and blue traction boots while a therapist encourages her.

"Come on, Starfish. You can sit. You can do it."

"Oh my goodness!" Leigh Anne exclaimed. She was thrilled with Starfish's dedication and determination. This little puppy had worked so hard and come so far in just a few short months!

STARFISH was rescued when she was around ten weeks old. This sweet Belgian Malinois puppy had a condition called swimmer puppy syndrome. The muscles in her inner thighs were so weak she couldn't stand up on her own.

The Gray family gave Starfish a home—
and a LOT of love.

When the
Gray family
first fostered
Starfish, she
had to wear a
diaper.

But Starfish was determined to stand—and walk—on her own!

The therapists at Berkeley's Holistic Veterinary Care and Rehabilitation Center fitted Starfish with pink booties to keep her from slipping on the floor.

Starfish made progress quickly. In just a few weeks she had a new blue harness.

The therapists and the Gray family used the harness to help Starfish get up on her feet.

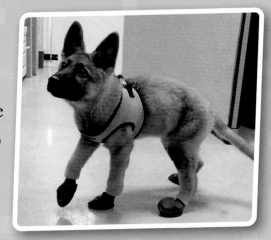

Soon Starfish was walking . . .

. . . and running!

When Starfish was six months old, she took her first hike with Oliver, Sarah, and Maggie.

Starfish has learned so much since her puppy days! She's outgrown her pink booties, her blue harness, and her name.

Today she's known as Rose.

Whether you call her Starfish or Rose, there's no doubt about one thing: This brave pup has shown the world what it truly means to never give up.

CHAPTER 9

A SURPRISE CALL

BRIIING! BRIIING!

Leigh Anne's phone rang. She answered it and sat down on the couch.

After chatting with the person on the other end for a while, she hung up and yelled.

Maggie, Sarah, and Oliver came running into the living room, followed by Liam.

"Is everything okay, Mom?" Maggie asked.

"Is it about Starfish?" Sarah wanted to know.

Leigh Anne shook her head. "You're not going to believe who just called."

The family just stood there looking at Leigh Anne.

"Come on, Mom," Maggie urged. "Tell us!"

"It was a producer from *The Dodo*!" Leigh Anne said.

"You mean the website where I watch those cute animal videos?" Maggie asked.

Leigh Anne nodded, a huge smile on her face. "That's right! They want to post a video of Starfish on their website."

"Really?!" Maggie asked. "That means tons of people will get to see Starfish and learn her story!"

Starfish barked. It seemed as though she was excited, too.

"Wow, that is amazing news," Liam said. "Is there anything we need to do to prepare for the video?"

Leigh Anne shook her head. "Right now, they're just going to compile their story from our videos and videos from FAAS and the rehab center."

"I have lots of good stuff on my phone they can use," Maggie offered.

"Me too!" Sarah added.

Maggie bent down and gave Starfish a big squeeze. "Starfish, soon the whole world will get to meet the amazing *you*!"

While the Gray family anxiously waited for *The Dodo*'s video to go live, Starfish continued her home therapy. And although Starfish wasn't having daily PT sessions anymore, she began working with a chiropractor at the rehab center, Dr. Lisa Koenig.

"I'm going to gently move Starfish's bones around," Dr. Koenig explained to Leigh Anne and Oliver during their first session.

"Please, don't break her," Oliver said, worry crossing his face.

Leigh Anne gave him a reassuring hug.

Dr. Koenig laughed. "Don't worry, Oliver. My treatment is good for Starfish. It will help line up her hips so that she can walk better."

A clearly relieved Oliver nodded his head and even managed a small smile.

After each treatment and therapy session, a video was posted on the rehab center's Instagram page. More and more people were seeing the videos and finding inspiration in Starfish's story and her hard work and dedication.

~

At home, Maggie and her family continued their hard work rehabilitating Starfish.

"Let's try going up the stairs," Maggie said as they placed Starfish at the bottom of the front steps to their house.

Starfish lifted up one leg. And then the other. Now, her two front legs were on the second step. But as she tried to lift up her hind legs, she tumbled backward!

"Starfish, are you okay?" Maggie ran over and swooped her up.

But Starfish was wagging her tail.

"I know you, Starfish," Maggie said. "You want to try again, right?"

And with that, Starfish headed up the stairs. This time, she made it to the top!

It was clear that Starfish had a ton of determination. She had no fear, and she never seemed to want to stop.

"You're my hero, Starfish," Maggie said, nuzzling the pup close. "And when *The Dodo*'s video comes out, you'll become a hero to people around the world!"

CHAPTER 10
THE VIDEO GOES VIRAL

"IT'S LIVE! IT'S LIVE!" MAGGIE called out one morning in April. "Starfish's *Dodo* video is up!"

The entire Gray family ran into Maggie's room and piled onto their bed to watch together.

Although the video was composed of

footage that the Grays, the shelter, and the rehab center had already seen, Leigh Anne had been interviewed for the voice-over.

The video began with Leigh Anne retelling the story of how Starfish was found and her initial diagnosis. Then it showed John Lipp, the director of FAAS, walking into the examination room. Leigh Anne explains how John insisted on getting a second opinion.

Maggie hugged Starfish close. "I'm so glad John saved you."

"Shh, Maggie!" Oliver said. "I can't hear the video!"

"When I saw Starfish, I just attached so quickly," Leigh Anne said. "You couldn't pick her up like you do a normal puppy. You had to hold her sideways. She was flat, like a pancake.

But I just grabbed her and didn't let her go." Leigh Anne's voice cracked with emotion as she remembered those early days.

Leigh Anne went on to explain that Starfish was diagnosed with swimmer puppy syndrome. "She moved like a swimmer—she moved like you would be doing the breaststroke."

"All we had to do was get her feet up underneath her," Leigh Anne said. "And as soon as we got her onto the grass and she had a little something to hold on to, she'd just follow us everywhere."

In the video, Leigh Anne went on to explain there was an entire team behind Starfish's recovery. "She had all these other people around her—the animal shelter folks who wanted to get her over to the rehab clinic. Those people knew what they were doing! She responded to everything that they taught her because she wanted it *so* bad."

As words of encouragement played on the video, Starfish wagged her tail.

"You were such a good girl through all of this," Maggie said.

"*Maggie . . .*" Oliver said.

"Okay, I'll be quiet," Maggie told her brother.

They watched as Leigh Anne continued to explain her experience with Starfish. "I don't usually walk into something like this with any expectation, or even any hope."

Maggie stopped the video. "Wait a minute, Mom. Are you saying that you didn't have hope for Starfish?"

Leigh Anne shook her head. "No. Exactly the opposite. There was something about

Starfish that *gave* me hope. Listen." Leigh Anne pressed the play button.

"The fact that she works at it so hard gives *me* hope," Leigh Anne said on the video. "She doesn't know what's wrong with her. She just gets up and does it again. And gets better, just a little bit, every single day. And *that's* the hope."

Maggie's eyes began to fill up with tears upon hearing their mom's words. Maggie vowed to show as much strength in their daily life as Starfish did.

Just then, Oliver started to giggle at the video clip. "Oh, I remember that! Starfish just walked right over to me and started to eat my french fries!"

Starfish's ears perked up. *Did someone say french fries?*

"I bet she could go for some right now," Sarah said.

"Actually, so could I," Liam said with a laugh.

"Sorry, it's not snack time," Maggie said as they focused their family's attention back to the video.

"Starfish, herself, was so determined at *every* moment to do whatever she could," Leigh Anne was saying in the video. "Whether it was walking down our steps for the first time—"

"I remember that!" Maggie said.

"I mean she, like, practically tumbled down, but she still did it again five minutes later," Leigh Anne's voice continued. "I knew that she would make progress because she just keeps going after it."

"Yay, Starfish!" Maggie shouted over the music swelling in the video.

"She was walking in two months!" Leigh Anne's voice continued. "Even when she's running across the lawn, it makes you want to drop to your knees like, 'Is this real?'"

Now Sarah was on-screen with Starfish.

"Yeah," Sarah said as she watched. "It really was unbelievable that this squished little puppy was running in such a short amount of time."

"Look, Maggie, it's you!" Oliver said, pointing to the screen.

Maggie was running with Starfish, with one end of a pull toy in their hand and the other in Starfish's mouth.

"She has a tremendous well of inspiration," Leigh Anne narrated over the video images.

"For us, this crazy family in the San Francisco Bay area, we need something grounding, and that's Starfish."

Leigh Anne was right; their family had really pulled together to help this puppy.

"Oliver, look! It's your turn." Maggie pointed to the screen. The video showed Oliver playing with Starfish.

"Maybe the most interesting relationship is with my five-year-old son," Leigh Anne said in the video. "Because they are kind of at similar developmental stages. They both are kind of floppy. They run around all goofy. They're chums. They're going to grow up together."

"I feel lucky that she came our way," Leigh Anne said as the video came to an end.

The entire family clapped and cheered.

"Well, now the entire world will know how special Starfish is," Liam commented.

"And I'm sure everyone will be inspired by her story," Leigh Anne added.

Maggie nodded, deep in thought. "You know, I think Team Starfish is about to get a whole lot of new members!" they said.

CHAPTER 11

A SETBACK

EVERY DAY, SOMEONE COMMENTED on Starfish's *Dodo* video. People were brought to tears. Some were inspired to work harder in their everyday lives. Others just left words of encouragement.

But then about a month after the *Dodo* video, Maggie noticed something was off with Starfish.

"Mom, have you noticed that Starfish has been walking a bit funny?" Maggie asked. "I feel like her hind legs are a little wobbly."

"What do you mean?" Leigh Anne asked. "It's not like her walking is one hundred percent okay. She still has some trouble."

Maggie shook their head. "No, this is different. Let's take her out for a walk and you'll see."

Maggie called for Starfish, leashed her up, and Maggie and their mom headed outside.

The sky was clear, and the sun shone on Starfish's brown coat. Maggie lifted their face, grateful that Alameda had beautiful weather year-round.

"Okay, I'll walk ahead of you with Starfish, and you let me know if you see something funny with the way she's walking," Maggie said to Leigh Anne.

After walking for a few minutes, Leigh Anne called out, "You're right Maggie. It's like she's limping. I've never seen her do that before."

Maggie stopped and looked at Leigh Anne, a concerned expression on their face. "Do you think we've been pushing her too hard? Do you think she's injured?"

"We won't know anything for sure until we take her to the vet," Leigh Anne said.

Maggie was worried. Starfish looked so happy, as usual. But what if Starfish was really hurt?

Maggie insisted on going with Starfish and their mom.

"Don't worry," Maggie said as they lifted Starfish into the car. "I'll be right by your side the whole time."

What should I be worried about, Maggie? Starfish thought. *Sure, I'm not walking very evenly, but my legs have always been a bit wonky. I should be telling* you *not to worry.* And with that, Starfish snuggled up to Maggie in the back seat.

When they arrived at the animal hospital, the receptionist enthusiastically greeted them as they walked through the door.

"Starfish!"

Starfish wagged her tail and walked over to get some treats.

"The doctor will be ready in a few minutes," the receptionist said.

In the examination room, the vet greeted

Starfish with a gentle pat on her head. "What can I do for one of my favorite patients today?"

Leigh Anne explained that they had noticed Starfish's rear hips wobbling more than usual, and that they were concerned.

"Hmm," the vet began.

"Do you think it's something really bad?" Maggie asked before the doctor could say anything else.

Their heart pounding, Maggie watched as the vet and the technician hoisted Starfish up on the table.

The vet gently moved Starfish's front leg around. As he did this, he had one hand on her hip. Then he moved her back leg around in the same way.

"Let's flip her over," the vet said to the technician.

Carefully, they flipped Starfish over so she was lying on her other side.

The vet did the same thing with Starfish's front and hind legs. Then he said she could come down off the table.

Maggie and Leigh Anne anxiously waited for a diagnosis.

"I'd like to take an X-ray of Starfish's hips," the vet said.

"Do you think something is wrong with her?" Maggie asked.

"I think there could be something wrong with her hip," the vet said. "But I need the X-ray to confirm it."

Maggie and Leigh Anne were ushered out to the waiting room. Leigh Anne tried to read a magazine while Maggie scrolled through their phone. But neither could concentrate.

At last, the vet came out to get them. "It's what I suspected. Starfish has severe hip dysplasia," the vet explained.

"Hip what?" Maggie asked.

The vet explained that Starfish's hip joints were not working the way they should be. Although this had been the case since Starfish's birth and her muscles were strong enough that she could walk now, the condition of her hips had gotten worse. With each step Starfish took, her hips popped in and out of joint.

"Is that dangerous?" Maggie asked.

"Well, it isn't very comfortable when your joints keep popping," the vet said. "And it's clearly affecting Starfish's walking."

Maggie nodded.

"But the good news is that this is a very

common condition in large dogs, and there's a surgery that can correct it," the vet continued. "The bad news is that she has the condition on two hips. So that means two surgeries."

"Surgery is scary," Maggie said.

"She's had a surgery before," Leigh Anne said, reminding Maggie about Starfish's hernia surgery. "And she came through that with flying colors!"

"True," Maggie said.

"This particular surgery is called femoral head ostectomy, or FHO," the vet said.

The vet went on to explain that the femoral head is the ball at the top of the femur bone. The femur is the long leg bone, or thighbone.

"During the operation, the surgeon will cut the ball of her femur off," the vet said.

"But then she'll have no ball and socket in

her hip," Maggie said. "How will she be able to walk?"

The doctor explained that Starfish's leg muscles would hold her femur in place.

"And the scar tissue that forms after her surgery will add extra support," the vet continued. "After she is feeling better from the first surgery, we'll do the second one. The surgeries will probably be about three weeks apart."

Maggie and Leigh Anne nodded. Although Starfish wouldn't have to start from square one like she did before, they both knew that there would be a lot of recovery time and rehab after the surgery. And Starfish would have to recover twice. But Team Starfish was ready to help her every step of the way!

"When do you think we should schedule the first surgery?" Leigh Anne asked.

"Just like with her rehab, the sooner the better," the vet said.

He handed Leigh Anne some paperwork, including the name of the surgeon, the veterinary hospital, and the cost of the operation.

When Leigh Anne saw how much the surgery would cost, she went pale.

How would Team Starfish ever be able to afford it?

CHAPTER 12

FUNDING STARFISH

WHEN THEY GOT HOME FROM THE vet's office, Leigh Anne pulled her phone out of her bag, walked into her bedroom, and shut the door. She needed to call John Lipp and give him an update.

"Hi, John, it's Leigh Anne."

"Hi, Leigh Anne," John answered. "Is everything okay with Starfish?"

"Well," Leigh Anne began. "I just came back from the vet, and it looks like she needs surgery on her hips. It's going to cost ten thousand dollars."

"That's a lot of money," John agreed.

"I don't want to worry the kids, especially Maggie, but I don't know how Team Starfish can afford to pay for that!"

"Don't worry, Leigh Anne," John tried to comfort her. "Let me talk it over with some people here. I'm sure we can find money in the Angel Fund to help."

Leigh Anne thanked John and hung up. And although she was thankful, as always, for John's help, she didn't want the burden of Starfish's surgery to fall totally on the Angel Fund.

What else could she do?

Just then, she heard a knock on her bedroom door. "Come in," Leigh Anne said.

It was Maggie, and they were holding Starfish.

"Mom, I can tell something's wrong," Maggie said. "Are you worried about Starfish's surgery?"

"In a way," Leigh Anne said.

"In what way?" Maggie wanted to know, sitting down on their mom's bed. Maggie put Starfish next to them.

"The surgery is going to cost a lot of money," Leigh Anne began. "And I don't want the burden of Starfish's surgery and recovery to fall on FAAS, financially. If they use all their money to help Starfish, they won't have much left to help other animals in need."

Maggie nodded with understanding.

Suddenly, they jumped up. "I know what we can do! We can start a GoFundMe page! Starfish already has a lot of fans and followers. I bet people will want to help!"

Leigh Anne hugged Maggie. "You are so smart! What would I do without you?"

Maggie laughed. "You should really be saying 'What would *Starfish* do without me?'"

Leigh Anne spoke with John and the rest of the team at FAAS. They all agreed that it was a good idea to start a GoFundMe page.

Leigh Anne got to work. She spent a lot of time writing about Starfish and asking if people could contribute money toward her surgery. She wrote and edited and rewrote. Finally, she felt that her words were perfect.

This is Starfish, she wrote under an adorable photo of the dog. *She was abandoned at ten weeks old on the beach in a box, unable to walk and splayed out on top of her food like a starfish . . . Starfish was born with swimmer puppy syndrome, a curable condition. Team Starfish was able to harness her indomitable spirit and guide her recovery . . .*

Leigh Anne went on to explain that now Starfish needed hip surgery.

Team Starfish supports this dog. Our continuing partnership with the nonprofit Friends of the Alameda Animal Shelter (FAAS)—the wonderful shelter that rescued Starfish, believed in her, and brought her into our lives—will accelerate Starfish's medical care. FAAS will be covering the costs of the surgeries and the follow-up care, which is estimated to be $10,000.

Please consider making a donation in honor of Starfish to help FAAS pay for her surgical procedures. The money from this campaign will be directed to their Angel Fund. Any funds raised in excess of what Starfish needs will help pay for the extraordinary medical care of other animals that come through the shelter—animals just like Starfish.

"Maggie, look!" Leigh Anne said soon after her post went live.

Maggie ran into the living room, where the rest of the family was gathered. They looked at their mom's computer: Donations to help Starfish had already started coming in!

"Everyone loves you so much," Maggie said, giving Starfish a giant hug. "So many people want to help you!"

Leigh Anne posted the GoFundMe page at

the end of April. Starfish's first FHO surgery was scheduled for May 1, 2018. The Gray family and FAAS were amazed that so many people donated money—and so quickly. This money would certainly take the burden off the shelter's Angel Fund.

"I can't believe the kindness of all these strangers," Leigh Anne said as the donations kept coming in and they approached their goal.

"Well, Starfish has certainly captured their hearts," Maggie said.

"Just like she captured ours," Liam added.

Leigh Anne wanted to keep the community involved in the time leading up to Starfish's surgery, so she posted updates on the GoFundMe page:

Starfish went on a long walk to the beach

today. Her puppy energy will allow for that kind of mobility right now. We're hoping that the first surgery (estimate cost: $5,000 for each surgery) will improve her mobility as well as relieve her pain. For now, though, we give her plenty of rest.

~~~

One day close to the surgery date, Oliver padded into Maggie's room and plopped on their bed—right next to Starfish.

"What if this time she can't be fixed?" Oliver asked.

"There's no question in my mind that the operation will be a success," Maggie said, ruffling Starfish's fur. "And she'll work hard in recovery, as usual!"

"But aren't you scared?" Oliver wanted to know.

"Of course I am," Maggie said. They gave

their little brother a tight squeeze. "But we have to be brave, just like Starfish. Right?"

After a moment, Oliver nodded. "Right!"

On April 30, 2018, Leigh Anne posted on the GoFundMe page that Starfish's surgery was the next day. And as soon as her post went up, Leigh Anne hoped that people around the world would be rooting for this little puppy that could.

CHAPTER 13

PUTTING STARFISH BACK TOGETHER AGAIN

ON THE DAY OF STARFISH'S FHO surgery, Maggie was awake before their alarm went off. Maggie felt jittery. Although they knew that Starfish would be fine, there was always a risk when an animal underwent surgery, right?

Starfish was fast asleep in her bed, hopefully

dreaming happy dreams. Maggie softly called her name, and Starfish woke up, her tail wagging.

"You have no idea what's going to happen today, do you?" Maggie said, ruffling Starfish's fur.

In response, Starfish gave Maggie about a million kisses!

When Maggie and Starfish came out of Maggie's bedroom, the rest of the family was at the dining table, already eating breakfast.

"Morning!" Maggie said, pulling out a chair.

Hey! Where's my food? Starfish wondered. *Usually we eat together. But today, not only did you start without me, but you also forgot to fill my bowl!* Starfish nudged her bowl with her nose and gave a small whine.

"Sorry, Starfish," Leigh Anne said,

putting the puppy's bowls up on the counter. "You can't have any food before your surgery. Doctor's orders!"

Starfish looked up at Leigh Anne with her dark brown eyes. *Please?*

Leigh Anne patted Starfish's head and returned to the table.

Soon, it was time to get ready to head to the VCA Bay Area Animal Hospital. Since it was a Tuesday, Maggie and Sarah had to be at school, and Liam had to go to work. So, just Leigh Anne and Oliver accompanied Starfish to the hospital.

"Don't forget to put on a jacket this morning, Oliver," Leigh Anne said. "It's a little chilly outside."

Oliver grabbed a jacket and then followed his mom and Starfish outside.

It was only about two and a half miles from the Grays' house to the hospital, so the car ride wasn't very long.

Leigh Anne parked and she, Oliver, and Starfish headed inside. They walked across the shiny floor, Starfish slipping a bit on the slick surface.

"Take it easy, girl," Leigh Anne said. "We don't want you to injure yourself even more before your surgery!"

After checking in at the front desk, Leigh Anne, Oliver, and Starfish sat in the waiting area.

Not long afterward, a nurse came to get Starfish.

"Good luck," Oliver said, giving Starfish a big kiss.

"We'll be waiting right here for you when you get out," Leigh Anne added.

And with that, Starfish was led into the operating room.

～～～

A few hours later, a nurse returned to the waiting room.

"Where's Starfish?" Oliver asked when he realized that the nurse was alone.

"She's out of surgery and in recovery," the nurse told Oliver and Leigh Anne.

"When do we get to see her?" Leigh Anne asked.

"We're going to keep her overnight in our ICU," the nurse said.

Oliver was confused. And scared. "What's an ICU?"

The nurse patted Oliver on the shoulder. "The ICU is the Intensive Care Unit," the nurse continued. "There, we will watch

Starfish around the clock. If she's in pain, we'll give her medicine. If she cries, we'll comfort her. Don't worry—I promise we'll take very good care of her."

Oliver nodded.

"Oliver, remember I told you that most people, and even dogs, stay overnight in the hospital after surgery?" Leigh Anne reminded her son.

"You did, but I really, really want her to come home," Oliver said. "Now."

"I'm sorry," Leigh Anne said, "But that's not possible. The best thing we can do for her is to let her stay here where the nurses can take care of her."

"Will they give her ice cream?" Oliver asked.

Leigh Anne laughed. "I don't think so. But

I'll tell you what: You can give her a treat when she comes home!"

As soon as Maggie returned from school that day, they wanted to know all the details about Starfish's surgery. Maggie sat down at the kitchen table, where Leigh Anne and Oliver filled them in on the day's events.

"The house is already so quiet without her," Maggie said. "I miss her."

Leigh Anne nodded. "We all do. But we can rest assured that Starfish is getting the best care tonight. And we get to pick her up tomorrow!"

Later that night, Leigh Anne updated Starfish's supporters on the GoFundMe page:

Starfish made it through surgery today, and she

is now recovering at VCA Bay Area Animal Hospital. We wanted to let you all know what's happening on the front lines of her medical care . . . She made it through the procedure, the work was double-checked with an X-ray, and now she is in their ICU . . . Now she will have three days on pretty heavy pain management and two to three weeks' recovery. We will keep in touch with photos and videos throughout her rehabilitation.

Leigh Anne shut down her computer and crawled into bed.

That night she dreamed about Starfish running along the beach. And when she woke up in the morning, Leigh Anne was smiling happily.

CHAPTER 14

ONE RECOVERY
IS NOT ENOUGH

"STARFISH, WHAT A FANCY COLLAR you have!" Maggie said when they went with their family to pick up Starfish from the hospital after school the next day.

What is this thing around my neck? It's not as stiff as the thing I had around my neck after my last surgery. This one is a lot softer. Still, can someone please get it off me?

The discharge nurse handed Leigh Anne instructions on how to care for Starfish at home.

"Just like after her last surgery," the nurse said, "it's important to watch the wound for any sign of infection. And she needs to keep the cone on until her stitches come out."

"At least the cone doesn't look too uncomfortable," Maggie said.

The nurse nodded. "Starfish will probably be in some pain, though, since this was an invasive surgery."

"What can we do to help her?" Maggie asked.

"It's all there in the papers I gave your mom, but for the first few days, Starfish will be on pain medication that will make her more comfortable."

"Can she walk?" Oliver wanted to know.

"Well, she did go out for a short walk this morning," the nurse said.

Maggie laughed. "Of course she did. Nothing can keep you down, Starfish, can it?"

"Not even major surgery!" Leigh Anne added.

"Still, it's best to keep her quiet and limit her activity for the next week," the nurse told them.

The Grays thanked the nurse, and Leigh Anne carried Starfish to the car.

"Ooof! You're getting heavy, Starfish. Luckily, I'm strong enough to carry forty pounds!" Leigh Anne said. "Good thing I had practice carrying you kids around!"

Maggie, Sarah, and Oliver laughed.

Once they got home, Leigh Anne gently lay

Starfish on her soft dog bed. "You take it easy, Starfish."

"That'll be hard for her to do," Maggie said. "I'm sure she's ready to start her rehab!"

Leigh Anne nodded. "I'm sure, too. But it's important to keep her calm for now. We'll all have to pitch in and make sure she doesn't get too excited."

Maggie bowed. "At your service, Starfish!"

As soon as Starfish was settled, Maggie started reading the discharge papers the vet had given them. Luckily, since Starfish had FHO surgery, her recovery wouldn't be as long as if she had a total hip replacement. The papers also explained that the head of Starfish's femur had been removed. Once a scar formed at the joint, Starfish would be free of pain.

But how would the scar form? Maggie

wondered. They read on and learned that the sooner Starfish began to use her leg, the faster the scar would develop and Starfish would begin to recover. Just like Starfish, Maggie was impatient for recovery to begin. But Maggie also knew that, for now, rest was the best medicine.

~~~

For the next few days, Starfish was so tired she didn't want to move.

This bed is so fluffy. And comfy. I don't think I ever want to . . . Starfish didn't get to finish her thoughts, because she had fallen asleep!

"I think it's time for Starfish's first post-surgery visit with Dr. Koenig," Leigh Anne told Maggie. Dr. Koenig was a chiropractor at the Holistic Animal Care and Rehabilitation Center. Starfish had seen her a few times before this surgery for adjustments. A chiropractic adjustment is when the spine or joints are moved around to help the body better align.

"But she's so sleepy," Maggie said. "I think she should still be resting."

"Remember what you read?" Leigh Anne said, reminding Maggie about the discharge instructions. "We have to get Starfish's body prepared for moving again. And Dr. Koenig is ready to help."

The next day, Leigh Anne carried Starfish to the car and placed her on a soft red-and-white blanket in the back seat.

When Leigh Anne arrived at the rehab center, she didn't take Starfish inside. Instead, she texted Dr. Koenig, who came outside to treat Starfish—it was a car call instead of a house call!

"Hello, Starfish," Dr. Koenig said, tucking her brown hair behind her ears. "How are you feeling?"

Starfish lay on the blanket but looked up at Dr. Koenig with eager eyes.

Dr. Koenig sat on the edge of the car's hatch and gently touched Starfish. Then she carefully wiggled her leg. *Pop!*

Starfish wagged her tail. It seemed as though the procedure had helped her feel better.

After a few minutes, Dr. Koenig turned to Leigh Anne.

"I was able to make some adjustments," she said. "That should help her feel a bit better."

"Thank you, doctor," Leigh Anne said. "See you in a couple of weeks."

Leigh Anne drove Starfish home and

carried her inside. She gently placed the dog back on her bed, where she promptly fell asleep. Healing after surgery was such hard work!

~

"Starfish, we're home!" Maggie called when they arrived home from school later that day.

Maggie and Sarah shrugged off their backpacks and ran over to Starfish's bed. The dog opened one sleepy eye.

"Mom, Starfish is way too heavy for me to lift now," Maggie called. "Can you help carry her into the living room? We want to play a game with her."

Leigh Anne brought Starfish into the living room where Oliver was waiting.

"Okay, Oliver, what game do you want to play?" Sarah asked her little brother.

"See these upside-down cups here?" Oliver asked.

Maggie and Sarah nodded.

"Well, all the cups are empty except for one," Oliver said. "One has a treat under it. And I want Starfish to guess which one."

Oliver carefully pushed the cups closer to Starfish.

Sniff, sniff, sniff. Starfish smelled each cup.

Then her tail started to wag. She knocked over one of the cups to reveal a treat.

"Good girl, Starfish!"

As Starfish continued to recover, the family hung out with Starfish in the living room since they really couldn't go outside to play. Sometimes they made up games for Starfish. Other times, they all snuggled up to watch a movie together.

As Starfish recovered, Leigh Anne continued to post videos and updates on the GoFundMe page. About two weeks after Starfish's surgery, Leigh Anne wrote:

We've been huddling low for too long! Starfish is starting to put weight on her hip, and I am starting to see the day when we can exercise her!

We've been restoring energy for the next surgery, due to take place in two weeks. Seems like such a terrible place for our sweet pup, and yet, the consensus among Starfish's team is to get the work done now while she's young. She'll have that much more time to work on her gait and get going as soon as the whole back end is fixed.

This experience is teaching us about interventions in an animal's life. Starfish is only about ten months old, and she's been through an incredible ordeal . . . Thank you for your notes of encouragement.

As Maggie read Leigh Anne's post, they gently hugged Starfish. "You've been so brave. And I know that whatever comes next, you'll make our family—and the world—so proud."

CHAPTER 15
THREE TIMES LUCKY

STARFISH'S SECOND HIP SURGERY— and third surgery in all—was scheduled only three weeks after her first FHO surgery. The Gray family felt bad about putting Starfish through surgery again so soon, but they knew it was the best thing to do. Without this surgery, Starfish would be in pain.

But for the days leading up to the surgery, Starfish was learning how to use her left leg again. And she was learning how to play with Pearl, the family's cat.

Come on, Pearl, let's play, Starfish thought. And this time, Pearl didn't arch her back or hiss or run away. *You really wanna play?* Starfish opened her mouth and playfully nipped the cat. And Pearl seemed to like it.

Now I'm going to pretend I'm eating you, Starfish thought. *Although I'm really not going to do that, of course! Oh, wait, there's the bouncy ball I also like to play with. See ya later, Pearl!*

Wait, thought Pearl, *where are you going, Starfish? I was just starting to like playing with you, and now you're running off! I'm going to get you . . .*

Playing with Pearl was helping Starfish

get stronger. Now she was able to take two walks a day.

"Starfish's left hip seems so much better," Maggie said as they returned from a walk.

"Yes," Leigh Anne agreed. "And even though she's going in for her next surgery tomorrow, I think her recovery will be easier since she now has one good leg to walk on."

At the sound of the word *surgery*, Maggie's heart sank. It made them so sad to think about Starfish enduring all that pain again. But Maggie knew it was for the best, and they vowed to be as strong as their beloved Starfish.

Two days after Starfish's second hip surgery, Leigh Anne posted this update on Starfish's GoFundMe page:

She is home again. I dropped her off yesterday,

feeling good that she would have her second hip repaired and feeling guilty to have to put her through another physical ordeal.

I don't know how dogs feel, but Starfish experiences all of this with grace. She is alert and her eyes are wary of any hands near her fresh incision, and she hops around looking for the cat. She wants to sit on her bed outside on this super windy night. She's the best. Her spirit is so strong.

The downside is that she has to be on a tether so she doesn't get into trouble as she heals. She has to wear a cushioned ring around her neck to discourage licking of her wound. She's on a bunch of meds for now.

The upside is that we get to start physical therapy in a few days! I am so psyched to start sending videos of this dog in action.

True to Starfish's can-do nature, only a week after her surgery, she was ready for rehab. Leigh Anne and Oliver took her back to the Holistic Veterinary Care and Rehabilitation Center.

The workers at the rehab center were overjoyed to see Starfish. And, from the looks of it, Starfish was pretty happy to be there, too. She greeted everyone with a joyful wag of her tail.

I'm back! Starfish thought. *How's everybody doing? Did you miss me? Now I have more work to do. But I promise to work hard!*

"It's important to start building Starfish's core and back leg strength," a therapist explained as she lay Starfish down on a mat.

Leigh Anne and Oliver listened closely.

The therapist continued, "There are two

types of stretches. There's an active stretch, where she'll use her muscle, and a passive stretch, where she'll be relaxed."

Oliver looked confused.

"Here, let me show you," the therapist offered. She took Starfish's hind leg and gently moved it backward.

"See, this is a nice stretch," the therapist explained. "Do you see how her back is lengthening? This is a passive stretch, since I'm doing the work and not Starfish."

Starfish raised her head, but the therapist convinced her to stay still by offering her a treat.

"If I just scratch her here," the therapist said, scratching Starfish's hip, "most dogs will think, 'Ah, this feels good,' and give a nice big stretch. I want Starfish to go into a hip stretch by herself."

The therapist continued to stretch Starfish's leg and followed that by scratching her hip. After a while, Starfish caught on and stretched out by herself!

"You are such a good girl, Starfish!" Leigh Anne encouraged her.

Then Leigh Anne looked up at the therapist. "Thank you for working with Starfish. I know with your expertise and Starfish's determination, she'll be up and running in no time at all!"

"Come on, Starfish," Leigh Anne called the next day. "It's time to get into the car!"

I'm so tired, Starfish thought. *I had such a hard workout yesterday. Can't I take the day off?*

Leigh Anne knew that Starfish was reluctant, but today she had a surprise for her.

Starfish stuck her nose out of the car window as Leigh Anne drove.

Sniff! Sniff! Hmm . . . this isn't the way to the rehab center. We're going to the shelter!

Starfish stood up and wagged her tail as Leigh Anne stopped the car and opened the back hatch. Alaina, the woman who had first rescued her, was standing in the parking lot!

Alaina! I've missed you! Starfish furiously wagged her tail back and forth. She couldn't wait for Leigh Anne to lift her up out of the car and onto the ground so she could give Alaina a million kisses.

But wait: There was something strange hanging off the car. *What's that for?*

"Starfish, you're getting a little too heavy for me to carry you," Leigh Anne explained, hoping Starfish would understand. "Plus, it's getting harder for me to control you when you get excited and try to wriggle out of my arms! So, Alaina brought us a ramp. Try to walk down it."

Starfish was certainly excited now, but at the same time, she was a little unsure.

"Come on, girl," Alaina encouraged from the bottom of the ramp. "You can do it!"

Starfish looked at Alaina and then back at Leigh Anne. She trusted these women with all her heart. She knew that they would never ask her to do something dangerous. *All right, Alaina: Here I come!*

And with that, Starfish scampered down the ramp.

"Good girl, Starfish!" Alaina said, folding her in a big hug.

"Thanks so much for lending us this ramp," Leigh Anne told Alaina. "It will be a big help getting Starfish in and out of the car for her therapy sessions. Soon, I'm sure we won't need it because Starfish will be jumping in and out of the car herself!"

~

While Starfish continued her work at the rehab center, the Gray family also worked with her at home to develop new skills.

"We have to get Starfish to turn her head," Leigh Anne explained to Maggie.

"But she can already do that, can't she?" Maggie asked.

"Yes, but we need her to do more twisting," Leigh Anne explained. "Watch."

Leigh Anne offered Starfish a treat, which she followed with her nose. When she twisted her head, Leigh Anne rewarded her with the treat.

"Following the treat with her nose forces her to stabilize her back end," Leigh Anne explained. "And the more stable her back end, the steadier she will be when she walks."

"Cool!" Maggie said.

Starfish wasn't only eager to walk steadier, she was also eager to walk fast—and even run. But moving too fast wasn't good for her hips just yet. So, to teach her to slow down her gait, Leigh Anne set up a row of cavalletti—the long poles—in the backyard. Going over the cavalletti taught Starfish to slow down as she moved.

Day after day, Starfish continued to grow stronger as Team Starfish cheered her on from the sidelines.

CHAPTER 16

STRENGTHENING STARFISH

AS STARFISH RECOVERED, THE GRAY family had to figure out how to keep her fit. And Leigh Anne had just the right idea: swimming! Now she had to find a place near their home in Alameda where Starfish could learn to swim.

Located in the Bay Area of San Francisco,

Alameda isn't just a city or an island—it's both! And since it's surrounded by so much water, Leigh Anne thought it might be a good idea to take Starfish swimming. Leigh Anne learned from Starfish's underwater treadmill therapy that water puts less pressure and strain on her joints. So, Leigh Anne thought swimming would be the perfect exercise for Starfish as she recovered from her surgeries.

Leigh Anne talked over her plan with her family.

"That's a good idea," Maggie said. "But remember, a lot of beaches around here don't allow dogs."

"But Starfish was found on a beach," Oliver said.

"True, but she couldn't exactly walk around then," Maggie told him.

"Why aren't dogs allowed on the beaches?" Sarah asked. "That seems like it would be the perfect place for them to run and have fun."

"A lot of birds make their nests on the Alameda shoreline," Leigh Anne explained. "And different species of migrating birds stop over there, too. So, dogs would just scare them, which wouldn't be good, since the beaches are the birds' safe spaces."

Oliver and Sarah understood.

"There are some rocky beaches where the birds don't go," Maggie suggested.

Leigh Anne shook her head. "But how would we get Starfish out to the water? She's too heavy to carry now, and the rocks are too slippery for her to walk on."

"True," Maggie agreed.

"And even if someone could carry her, it

would be slippery for them, too," Sarah added.

"Well, there are two spots in town that are publicly owned and have boat ramps that Starfish can walk on to reach the water," Leigh Anne said.

The family agreed that could work. Operation Swimming Starfish was a go!

~~~

A few days later, Leigh Anne and Oliver led Starfish to the boat ramp. *Whoa!* Starfish thought as her legs slipped and slid from underneath her. *What is this green slippery stuff?*

"It looks like Starfish is having a hard time walking on the seaweed," Leigh Anne observed.

Just then, Oliver pulled something out of his pocket.

A squeaky ball! I love squeaky balls! Throw it to me, Oliver! Please!

But instead of tossing the ball to Starfish, Oliver threw the ball into the water.

As Oliver raised his arm to throw, a frightening thought crossed Leigh Anne's mind: What if Oliver threw the ball too far out, where the current was strong? Then Starfish might be carried out into the San Francisco Bay!

But when Leigh Anne saw that Oliver's small arm didn't have much of a reach, she breathed a sigh of relief.

However, Starfish wasn't happy. *I want that ball. Now how am I going to get it?*

Starfish thought for a moment and then . . . *Here goes!* She ran into the bay!

"Good girl, Starfish!" Oliver called out. "Get your ball!"

"And swim!" Leigh Anne added, silently

hoping she wouldn't have to go into the water to rescue her dog from the waves.

Sure enough, Starfish dog-paddled over to the ball and grabbed it in her mouth. Then she swam back to the ramp.

"Look!" Oliver exclaimed. "Starfish can swim!"

After her first lesson, Leigh Anne and Oliver brought Starfish back to the boat ramp several times a week. Each time, Oliver threw the ball a little farther out—but not *too* far. And each time, Starfish swam out to retrieve it, huffing and puffing when she got back to the shore.

One day, after Oliver had thrown the ball about five times, Starfish lay down on the sand. *I'm pooped*, she thought.

Leigh Anne and Oliver were proud of

Starfish for working so hard. And they knew that this exercise was helping her get in shape. But they also knew when enough was enough, so they turned around and headed home.

~

As Starfish grew stronger, the Gray family took her on longer and longer walks. Hopefully, the walks would help her develop other muscles in her legs.

One day, they took Starfish on a dirt trail that led up a hill. The day was crisp, and the sun bounced off the trees.

"Starfish has never been here before, so I'm going to hold her leash tight," Leigh Anne told her children.

Usually, Starfish was excited on her walks, but this time she seemed a little unsure. Leigh Anne had to encourage her to keep up.

I'm coming, I'm coming. Starfish's legs shivered as her paws tried to grasp the unfamiliar dirt beneath her.

"Why is she walking so slowly?" Oliver asked.

"Even though she's getting stronger, her body still isn't like every other dog's," Maggie reminded him.

Oliver nodded.

I think I have this, Starfish thought after walking for a while. *I can . . .*

Starfish didn't finish her thought because a small, furry creature dashed across the path. Excitedly, Starfish tugged on her leash. *What was that? Was that Pearl? I didn't know she was coming along!*

"What did you see, Starfish?" Sarah asked. "A little rabbit?"

Leigh Anne let go of Starfish's leash and the dog followed the rabbit's scent. But the rabbit had already hidden itself safely away in some brush.

I'll get you to play with me next time! Starfish thought.

～～～

One of Starfish's favorite hikes was at the Sunol Wilderness Regional Preserve. The preserve has over two hundred miles of trails, which provided Starfish plenty of space to run around.

One day, Leigh Anne and Oliver decided to walk Starfish along a creek bed for a couple of miles. By this time, not only had Starfish become a better hiker, but so had Oliver.

Leigh Anne breathed in the fresh, crisp air as Oliver ran ahead. All around them were low-growing grass and green trees. Ahead, they could see grass-covered hills.

And although Starfish had run off the trail a bit, Leigh Anne was confident that she wouldn't go too far. Plus, she was always in eyesight of them.

"Is it time for lunch yet?" Oliver asked after they had only been walking a short time.

Leigh Anne laughed. "No, but you can have a snack."

After a few minutes, Oliver stopped again. "Can I climb that tree? Please?"

"Okay, but after that we need to keep going, otherwise we'll never get to the top of the creek."

Oliver scurried off.

Meanwhile, Starfish was having fun of her own. The cool grass felt so good under her paws, and there were always new things to find. *Hello there,* Starfish said to a worm that was wiggling along a rock. *Are you having a good hike today? I know I am!*

When it was time for lunch, Leigh Anne told Oliver the story of the people who this land belonged to, the Ohlone. The Ohlone were made up of different groups, or tribes, who lived in different villages and spoke different languages. They built circular homes near the water out of reed, grass, and poles.

"Why do you think they lived near the water?" Leigh Anne asked.

"So they could fish?" Oliver said.

"Exactly!" Leigh Anne said.

"Tell me more," Oliver said.

Leigh Anne looked at her watch. "I think we should pack up here and continue our hike. When we get home, we'll take out some books from the library and learn more about the Ohlone."

Oliver nodded and ran off with Starfish.

Soon, the sun began to dip in the sky, and the air cooled. Leigh Anne zipped up her hoodie and shivered a bit, worried that they wouldn't make it back down the trail before it got too dark.

Suddenly, Leigh Anne noticed that a herd of cows who ranged freely in the area had started to come down the hills that sloped toward the creek. If she, Oliver, and Starfish didn't move quickly, they would be surrounded!

Who are you? Starfish thought as the cows moved closer and closer. *You walk on four legs like a dog, but you aren't dogs or cats.*

Just then, Leigh Anne secured the leash

around Starfish's collar. "Come on, Starfish, we have to get moving!"

"Do you mean *moo-ving*?" Oliver asked.

"That's funny, Oliver," Leigh Anne said. "But we could be in trouble if we get too close to the herd. They don't know who we are, and they may think we will hurt them."

"But we won't," Oliver said.

"We know that, but the cows don't," Leigh Anne explained. "So it's best to keep our distance."

The cows were even closer now.

"Mom . . ." Oliver started.

Leigh Anne shushed him, not wanting to frighten the cows.

For the remainder of the hike, Leigh Anne held tightly to Oliver with one hand, and to Starfish's leash with the other.

Wow, we're really hiking fast today! Starfish thought. *But I can keep up! What an adventure!*

They walked like this until they were back at their car as the darkness settled around them. It was time to head home.

CHAPTER 17
THE DODO—AGAIN!

JANUARY BROUGHT A NEW YEAR for the Gray family—filled with joy, hope, and surprises! Early one morning, Leigh Anne's cell phone rang. She excitedly spoke on the phone as the family sat around the kitchen table wondering who was on the other end.

"Well, that was a surprise!" Leigh Anne said as she hung up her phone.

"Is it about Starfish?" Oliver asked.

Leigh Anne nodded. "She's part of it."

"Was it the TV station wanting to come film her for a story?" Sarah wondered aloud.

"Filming is part of it," Leigh Anne said.

"We give up!" Maggie said, clearing the breakfast plates from the table. "Just tell us!"

"It was a producer from *The Dodo*," Leigh Anne began.

"Again?" Maggie asked. "We already did a video with them last March. That's almost a year ago."

"But this one would be different—and longer," Leigh Anne said. "They want to film Starfish for an episode of their *Comeback Kids* series."

Maggie pulled out their phone and scrolled through it until they found some information on the series. "It says here that 'These animals had a rough start in life—until they found someone who refused to give up on them.'"

"That would be us!" Sarah said.

"That's true," Leigh Anne said. "But with this video, *The Dodo* producer wants to focus on the bond between Maggie and Starfish. He said that from the first video it was clear that you and Starfish are very close."

Maggie blushed. "Why just me? Why not the rest of the family?"

"You have to admit that what you and Starfish have is pretty special, right?" Leigh Anne said. "You were the one who took care of Starfish when we fostered her. And you convinced us to adopt her. Plus, you took such good care of her after her surgeries!"

"I guess so," Maggie said, giving Starfish an extra-special hug. "So, when do we start?"

"They'll schedule a film crew to come to the house in a couple of weeks," Leigh Anne said. "I should get more details soon."

Later that night, with Starfish cuddled up in their bed, Maggie said, "Can you believe it, Starfish? We're going to be *stars*!"

~

Buzz! Buzz!

Maggie rolled over and shut off the alarm. They cracked open one eye. *It's still dark out. Why should I get out of bed?* Then Maggie realized it was the day of the *Comeback Kids* filming. They quickly scrambled out of bed and got dressed.

When Maggie came into the kitchen, their

parents were already at the kitchen table. And Starfish was eating her breakfast.

"Ready for your big day?" Leigh Anne asked Maggie.

"I hope so!" Maggie said.

Just then, the doorbell rang.

"I'll get it!" Maggie said cheerfully as they opened the front door for the *Dodo* team.

The producer handed Maggie a box of doughnuts. "Hi, I'm Cali," she said. "I brought you an early morning present."

"Thanks! I'm glad I didn't eat breakfast yet!" Maggie said.

Maggie led Cali inside. They looked around for Oliver and Sarah. They were probably still sleeping. But as soon as Maggie announced that there were doughnuts, the rest of the family quickly appeared.

Soon, Cali, a camera operator, and a sound person had all crowded into the small house. Cables, cords, and cameras were everywhere. There was *so* much equipment.

"Okay, time to get Maggie, Leigh Anne, and Liam fitted with mics," the sound guy said.

He handed each of them a box and showed them how to clip on the mic and run its wire up below their chins, where it was taped down and hidden from view of the cameras.

"Perfect!" the sound guy said when they were done. "Now we can easily pick up what you say in your interviews. Maggie, you're up first."

"Okay, what do you want me to do?" Maggie asked.

"I'm going to ask you some questions," Cali

said. "Try not to stare directly into the camera when you're speaking. It'll feel more natural that way."

Maggie nodded.

"Tell me about your connection to Starfish and a bit about how you feel about her," Cali began.

"We had this instant connection," Maggie said. "She was always trying to stand up, always. She never stopped. When Starfish first walked, I started to cry because it felt like a miracle to me. I don't even know how she did it. She just kept trying over and over again. I feel like I'm a mom watching my little kid learn how to walk."

"That's perfect, Maggie!" Cali said.

After interviewing Maggie, it was Leigh Anne and Liam's turn. They sat in the living room and answered the questions like pros.

When the interviews were complete, the crew started to pack up.

"Is that it?" Maggie asked. "Don't you want more?"

"Sure we do," Cali said. "That's why we're all heading outside!"

The crew and the Gray family went to shoot footage at some of Starfish's favorite places. First, they went to the dog park, where Starfish romped around with one of her friends.

Tag, you're it! Starfish nosed her friend as they played and then she ran off, waiting to be tagged herself.

The next stop was a beautiful location in San Francisco overlooking the ocean. The day was a bit overcast, but Maggie's and Starfish's spirits were high. As Maggie lifted Starfish out of the car, some of Maggie's friends were there to greet them.

Yay! Starfish thought. *More friends to play with!*

Starfish ran along the sand, her paws leaving deep footprints. And, of course, she swam. Oh, how she loved to swim! And as Maggie pointed out, it was kind of ironic that a dog who was born with swimmer puppy syndrome now loved the water so much!

By the end of the day, the entire family was exhausted, especially Starfish. That evening she curled up in her bed and didn't stir again until morning.

On March 28, 2019, a year and a half after her rescue, Starfish's episode of *Comeback Kids* went live.

The Gray family settled down in their living room to watch, a big bowl of popcorn on the table and Starfish lying at their feet.

"I'm too nervous to watch," Maggie said, covering their eyes.

"Don't be silly," Leigh Anne said, pulling down Maggie's hands. "You're going to be great!"

The video began with Starfish's rescue and went on to cover her rehabilitation. Between the clips, the episode showed the interviews from Maggie, Leigh Anne, and Liam.

"Starfish's attitude throughout this whole thing was relentless. It never occurred to her to stop," Leigh Anne said in the video.

As Leigh Anne watched and listened to her own words, she patted Starfish affectionately.

The family watched as they heard Maggie's inspirational interview: "Sometimes when I'm on a difficult math problem, I'll think, *you know, Starfish couldn't walk, and she stood up and basically taught herself. I think I can do this math problem!*"

Not only did Starfish "help" Maggie with their homework, Starfish also supported them through their teenage years.

"My relationship with Starfish definitely makes me a better and happier person," Maggie said in their interview. "This was the first time that I had so much responsibility with a dog. Seeing a dog that's been through so much and is still so happy with her life and getting to see her like this is the best feeling in the world."

But Liam really summed up what Starfish has meant to him and his family and their friends. He told *The Dodo*, "She's really in love with life. And it's really impossible to be around her and not just see it but feel it. Starfish really wants to live and doesn't care about the obstacles . . . If we could all have that attitude, the world would be a completely and totally different place."

When the video ended, Maggie was in tears.

"Why are you crying, Maggie?" Oliver asked.

"It's just that now I totally realize that not only did I help Starfish, but she helped me. She helped all of us by showing us how to be determined and never, ever give up. I call that a great life lesson!"

"Group hug!" Sarah shouted as she gathered everyone together—including Starfish!

CHAPTER 18

EPILOGUE

TODAY, STARFISH IS STILL THE SAME lovable dog with the same can-do attitude, but she's no longer called Starfish. Her name is Rose.

Why this name?

Maggie, Sarah, and Oliver all love the animated television show *Steven Universe*. They named their cat, Pearl, after one of the characters, because in the show Pearl has an attitude, just like their cat.

Rose was named for the character Rose Quartz. This character is compassionate, loving, and everyone wants to be around her—just like their dog!

These days, Rose really doesn't like going on long walks. When Leigh Anne takes her out, Rose just curls up on the ground after a quarter block. Somehow, Leigh Anne is always able to coax Rose back home.

But Rose loves the dog park, especially when she sees friends who she can play with! And of course, Rose still loves to swim. Swimming puts less pressure on her joints and makes her feel free. Anytime Oliver tosses a ball into the San Francisco Bay, Rose dashes in right after it!

Even though Rose goes by a different name now, "Team Starfish" continues to grow bigger and bigger each day. Her *Comeback Kids* video has tens of millions of views from across the world! One woman in England sold clothing so she could donate money to help with "Starfish's" care. And a soldier keeps the dog's photo folded inside his cap for inspiration as he trains.

Inspiration: That's what Starfish has spread. So many people know what it's like to go through a tough time, even when there's a good time on the other side. So when they saw Starfish going through struggles and successes, they really *felt* for her. If Starfish could do it, so could they! Starfish never gave up, and she showed people how that kind of attitude has a way of making life bigger and better than anything they could have imagined.

MORE ABOUT FRIENDS OF THE ALAMEDA ANIMAL SHELTER

An animal shelter is a place where lost, abandoned, abused, or surrendered animals are temporarily housed and cared for. But Friends of the Alameda Animal Shelter (FAAS) isn't your ordinary animal shelter. While FAAS does provide care for lost and surrendered animals, it also provides other services:

- Access to low-cost spay and neuter services to help keep the animal population down

- Low-cost and free services to families who can't afford to care for their pets
- Educational programs for young people and adults on how to treat their pets with love and kindness
- Dog training classes and recommendations for other behavioral services
- Foster and adoption services

FAAS opened its doors in 2009 as an all-volunteer support group to raise money for the local city shelter. When budget cuts threatened to close the shelter in 2012, FAAS stepped forward and began managing the shelter. Since 2017, FAAS has been able to save 95 percent of the one thousand animals that are brought to it each year.

Today, FAAS views itself as a community

center where spaying and neutering, training, fostering, and adoption are all conducted under one roof. In addition, it has a dedicated space for school groups, afterschool programs, and partnerships with youth service organizations that teach the values of showing kindness and respect toward animals. Hands-on learning at the center helps keep both kids and animals safe. FAAS even has a space for birthday parties!

Starfish still holds a special place in the hearts of the people at FAAS. When Starfish was in need, FAAS used money from its Angel Fund to pay for her care and surgeries. And to honor this special dog, it renamed the Angel Fund the Starfish Fund.

For more information, check out its website: https://www.alamedaanimalshelter.org.

HOW TO HELP DOGS
AT AN ANIMAL SHELTER

There are many ways in which you can help your local animal shelter. Some things you can do on your own, while others may require help from an adult:

VOLUNTEER

Shelter volunteers can do many jobs: walk dogs, refill water bowls, give out treats, and simply play with the dogs to help them get used to people before being fostered or adopted. Sharing your love with animal shelter residents goes a long way! Many shelters require volunteers to be a certain age, so you might need to wait a few years or ask for an adult to join you.

RAISE MONEY

Your local animal shelter probably needs money to buy supplies, build enclosures, and more. Here are some ways you might raise money to donate to your local shelter:

- Organize a lemonade sale or bake sale in a public place, like outside your house, in front of your school, or even at the library. Be sure to get permission from the place you're selling before setting up, and always talk to an adult before organizing anything. To make your bake sale extra special, try creating some dog-shaped treats!

- Set up a dog wash! You can do this in your driveway, backyard, or in front of your house. Ask local stores to donate supplies like dog soap, brushes, towels, etc. Pet owners can bring their pets for a bath and leave a donation in return!

- Make a pet calendar by taking pictures of some of the cutest animals you know. There are online companies you can use to create and print your calendar. You can donate your profits from the sale of your calendar to a local shelter.

COLLECT OLD BLANKETS AND SHEETS

When dogs are brought into a shelter, they are usually shivering from the cold or out of fear.

In these cases, there is nothing like being wrapped up in a cozy blanket or sheet. Ask friends and family members if they have any extra bedding, then bring clean donations to the animal shelter. (Make sure you call first to make sure they are currently accepting donations.)

IS YOUR FAMILY READY TO FOSTER A DOG?

Fostering a dog means giving a homeless animal a temporary place to live. Many shelters are overcrowded, so fostering a dog frees up space for other animals. By fostering, you can give it a safe and less stressful place to live until the animal is able to move to a forever home.

Taking a dog into your home and offering them love and shelter is rewarding. But it's also hard work. Some animals need fostering for a few days while others need a place to stay for a few months. Here are some questions to ask your family to see if you're ready to foster:

- Why do you want to help a shelter dog? Do you love dogs? Does every member of your family feel the same way?

- Do you have enough space in your home? Is there a yard where the dog can run around? Can you easily, and safely, let the dog outside by itself? Or is there a place near your house where you can walk the dog?

- Do you have the time to care for a foster dog? Will someone be home during the day to walk the dog? If not, can your family hire a dog walker? Do you have enough time between schoolwork and after-school activities to take care of and play with a dog?

- Are you ready to help train the shelter dog? Training takes a lot of time and patience!

If you decide to foster a dog, you will have to dog-proof your home to keep the dog safe. Here are some things you may need to do:
- Remove small objects from the floors and tables
- Keep electrical cords out of reach
- Cover trash cans
- Install childproof latches on cabinets and toilets
- Keep plants out of reach

Fostering a dog can be challenging, but it's worth it. All the love you give will be returned to you one hundred times over! And when it's time for the dog's adoption, it can be hard to say goodbye. What makes it SO worth it is seeing how happy your foster dog is with their forever family. Be sure to ask the dog's family to send you pics all the time! And once your foster pup is adopted, that means there's room in your house to foster another dog in need—if your parents say yes again.